AF760036

CONTENTS

PREFACE

This book discusses these options and strategies in detail, while also providing defined contribution plans and examining income replacement during retirement years in these defined contribution plans.

Chapter 1 - American workers are primarily saving for retirement through their 401(k) plans and will likely need assistance making complicated decisions about how to spend their money throughout retirement. Other countries with defined contribution (DC) systems are also dealing with this spend-down challenge. To identify lessons for the U.S. from the experiences of other countries, GAO examined selected countries' (1) approaches to offering retirement spend-down options; (2) strategies to help participants make sound decisions; and (3) approaches to regulating and overseeing options. An initial review of countries with established DC systems indicated that some countries including the six GAO selected—Australia, Canada, Chile, Singapore, Switzerland, and the United Kingdom—have developed innovative spend-down policies that have the potential to yield useful lessons for the U.S. experience. GAO reviewed reports on DC plans; and interviewed experts and government officials in the U.S. and selected countries.

Chapter 2 - Service providers play important roles in the U.S. defined contribution (DC) retirement system since they provide services, such as administration and fund management, necessary for operating DC plans. Plan sponsors rely on such providers, yet it is unclear how much participants are paying in fees for these services. Other countries with well-established DC systems face similar issues and some use a variety of approaches to oversee DC plans and service providers and actively focus on fees charged to participants.

GAO was asked to examine, for selected countries' DC systems, (1) how are service providers overseen by regulatory agencies; (2) what key strategies are used to improve fee disclosure to participants; and (3) what key strategies are used to reduce fees? GAO selected Australia, Chile, Sweden and the United Kingdom based on, among other factors, the importance of the DC plans to the country's retirement system and the use of strategies to address service providers' fees. GAO reviewed research on DC plans; collected and analyzed available data; and interviewed government officials, pension experts, service providers, and other relevant representatives in the U.S. and selected countries.

Chapter 3 - The 2012 ERISA Advisory Council (the Council) examined income replacement during retirement years in a defined contribution retirement system and the issues individuals and plan sponsors face to ensure financial security during the participants' retirement years. In the past, the challenge of providing retired employees with a source of income to last during their retirement was primarily met through a source of lifetime income provided by employer-sponsored defined benefit pension (DB) plans. To that end, DB plans typically offered an annuitized benefit to participants. The responsibility of providing such a lifetime benefit was that of the plan sponsor through the design of the plan. However, the continued shift from DB plans to defined contribution (DC) plans as a primary source of retirement income has shifted the burden of providing a continued stream of income during the retirement years of DC plan participants. As a result of this shift there is a growing need for plan sponsors to examine, evaluate and make available to participants, options designed to address their retirement income needs in a DC plan context. In addition, there is a need to sufficiently educate participants so that they can fully understand the importance of viewing and analyzing their account balances as a source of lifetime income. The Council believes that this education will better equip participants to exercise meaningful choices with regards to their continued financial security during retirement.

The purpose of the Council's examination of this issue is to provide recommendations to the Department of Labor (DOL) on guidance for plan sponsors and participants at a time that this topic is being highlighted among pension experts, and the market is beginning to respond with innovative products. Examination of the issue focused on the following: (1) the challenges participants face in making their account balances last for the length of their retirement years, especially in light of improved longevity; (2) what options and resources should be available to participants to help them in their efforts to transform their accumulated savings into a continued flow of income designed to last over their retirement lives and/or the lives of their spouses; (3) what considerations and/or challenges plan sponsors encounter when making these options available to plan participants; and (4) what considerations and challenges face plan sponsors in providing education outreach for participants of DC plans regarding available income replacement options.

Through testimony and research, the Council developed recommendations to the Secretary that certain plan sponsors and participants may find beneficial when examining options for income replacement in a DC plan system. Specifically, the recommendations in this report include enhancing regulatory and sub-regulatory guidance that may help plan sponsors address their fiduciary concerns when offering income replacement options or advice on available options, and the development of educational/outreach materials for both plan sponsors and participants to result in a greater chance of DC participants achieving lifetime income in retirement.

In: 401(k) Plans and Spend-Down Options
Editor: Erica L. Chapmann
ISBN: 978-1-63117-580-0

Chapter 1

401(K) PLANS: OTHER COUNTRIES' EXPERIENCES OFFER LESSONS IN POLICIES AND OVERSIGHT OF SPEND-DOWN OPTIONS*

United States Government Accountability Office

WHY GAO DID THIS STUDY

American workers are primarily saving for retirement through their 401(k) plans and will likely need assistance making complicated decisions about how to spend their money throughout retirement. Other countries with defined contribution (DC) systems are also dealing with this spend-down challenge. To identify lessons for the U.S. from the experiences of other countries, GAO examined selected countries' (1) approaches to offering retirement spend-down options; (2) strategies to help participants make sound decisions; and (3) approaches to regulating and overseeing options. An initial review of countries with established DC systems indicated that some countries including the six GAO selected—Australia, Canada, Chile, Singapore, Switzerland, and the United Kingdom—have developed innovative spend-down policies that have the potential to yield useful lessons for the U.S. experience. GAO reviewed reports on DC plans; and interviewed experts and government officials in the U.S. and selected countries.

* This is an edited, reformatted and augmented version of the United States Government Accountability Office publication, GAO-14-9, dated November 2013.

WHAT GAO RECOMMENDS

GAO recommends that DOL and Treasury, as part of their ongoing efforts, consider other countries' approaches in helping 401(k) plan sponsors expand access to a mix of spend-down options for participants. GAO also recommends that DOL consider other countries' approaches in providing information about options and regulating the selection of annuities within DC plans. In response, DOL generally agreed with GAO's recommendations and will evaluate approaches.

WHAT GAO FOUND

The six countries GAO reviewed can offer U.S. regulators lessons on how to expand access to a mix of spend-down options for 401(k) participants that meet various retirement needs. Five of the six countries generally ensure that participants can choose among three main plan options: a lump sum payment, a programmed withdrawal of participants' savings, or an annuity. In the last several decades, all the countries took steps to increase participant access to multiple spend-down options, with some first conducting reviews of participants' retirement needs that resulted in policy changes, as shown below. In the United States, 401(k) plans typically offer only lump sums, leaving some participants at risk of outliving their savings. The U.S. Departments of Labor (DOL) and the Treasury (Treasury) have begun to explore the possibility of expanding options for participants, but have not yet helped plan sponsors address key challenges to offering a mix of options through their plan.

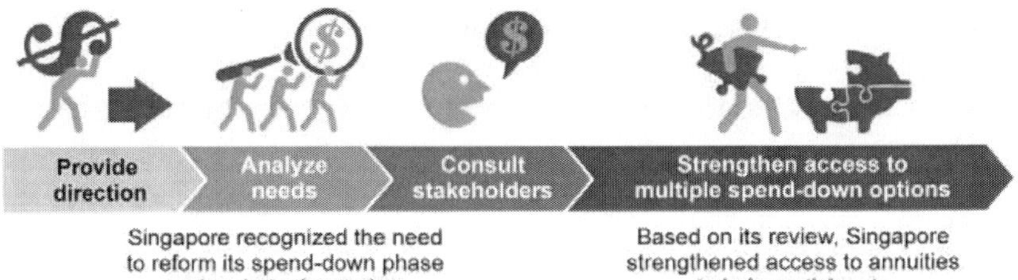

Source. GAO analysis of documents from Singapore's National Longevity Insurance Committee and Central Provident Fund.

Note: GAO did not conduct an independent legal analysis of the laws, regulations, or policies of the countries selected for this study.

Example of Steps Taken by Other Countries to Strengthen Access to Multiple Spend-down Options.

Countries reviewed used various strategies to increase participants' knowledge and understanding of spend-down options, which may be useful to DOL in its ongoing efforts. Strategies used by other countries include (1) communicating spend-down options to participants in an understandable and timely manner, and (2) helping participants see how their savings would translate into a stream of income in retirement by providing them with projections of retirement income in their annual benefit statements. Currently, 401(k) participants have difficulty predicting how long their savings will last because most benefit statements do not focus on the stream of income it can generate. DOL is currently considering including income projections in statements, which may help participants better understand what their balance could provide on a monthly basis once they retire.

Regulators in the countries GAO reviewed employed several approaches to overseeing the spend-down phase aimed at helping participants sustain an income throughout retirement. For example, most of the countries used withdrawal rules and restrictions for lump sums and programmed withdrawals to help protect participants from outliving their savings. With respect to annuities, DOL continues to consider current regulatory barriers that may prevent 401(k) plan sponsors from offering annuities, which do not exist in other countries. Looking at what other countries require may help DOL in its efforts.

ABBREVIATIONS

ABI	Association of British Insurers
AFP	Administradoras de Fondos de Pensiones
APRA	Australian Prudential Regulatory Authority
CPF	Central Provident Fund
DB	defined benefit
DC	defined contribution
DOL	Department of Labor
EBSA	Employee Benefits Security Administration
ERISA	Employee Retirement Income Security Act of 1974

FIO	Federal Insurance Office
IRS	Internal Revenue Service
NAIC	National Association of Insurance Commissioners
OECD	Organisation of Economic Co-operation and Development
Treasury	Department of the Treasury
U.K.	United Kingdom

November 20, 2013

The Honorable George Miller
Ranking Member
Committee on Education and the Workforce
House of Representatives

The Honorable Robert E. Andrews
Ranking Member
Subcommittee on Health, Employment, Labor and
Pensions Committee on Education and the Workforce
House of Representatives

American workers are primarily saving for retirement through 401(k) plans, which have become the dominant type of plan private sector employers are offering in the United States.[1] Since the inception of 401(k) plans, regulators have focused their efforts on ensuring that plan participants accumulate savings for retirement.[2] With many participants who have had defined contribution (DC) plans throughout their career nearing retirement, regulators have begun to focus on the decumulation phase, or the spending down of retirement savings, because of the real possibility that some retirees may outlive their savings. Unlike participants in traditional defined benefit (DB) plans who are offered a specific periodic benefit for life at retirement, 401(k) plan participants must take responsibility for the complex decisions required in the spend-down phase. By 2015, participants whose retirement savings will be primarily made up of what they accumulated in their 401(k) plans, which were introduced in 1978, will be eligible to retire. Typically, 401(k) plan participants receive benefits as a lump sum payment and are thus primarily left on their own to manage their money in a way that ensures they do not outlive their retirement savings.[3] Current regulatory efforts by the Department of Labor (DOL) and the Department of the Treasury (Treasury) have begun to focus on the spend-down phase as it has become clearer that workers in the United States are increasingly subject to financial risks in retirement that can cause them to either outlive their savings or to lower their standard of living.

The United States is not alone in facing this growing concern for retirees. Other countries with retirement systems dominated by DC plans similar to 401(k) plans face the same problem of ensuring that plan participants effectively manage the spending of their retirement savings, whether under a mandatory or voluntary system. This is particularly important given the common challenges of low average balances of DC plan participants and the longer average life expectancies.[4]

Some countries have developed innovative approaches and strategies that can help participants better manage their DC plan savings throughout their lives, while the United States has just begun to explore ways to help 401(k) plan participants. As DOL and Treasury move forward, you expressed interest in potential lessons learned from countries that have addressed these issues. This report addresses the following questions:

1. What approaches have other countries with DC plans taken to offer participants certain retirement spend-down options?
2. What key strategies are used in other countries with DC plans to help participants make sound spend-down decisions to improve retirement outcomes?
3. What approaches have other countries used to regulate and oversee spend-down options?

To answer these questions, we selected six countries with extensive or growing DC systems in which to conduct in-depth reviews of retirement spend-down phase strategies: Australia, Canada, Chile, Singapore, Switzerland,[5] and the United Kingdom (U.K.). We selected these countries from an initial review of countries with well-developed account based retirement systems.

In selecting these six countries, we considered if the country had (1) developed innovative spend-down phase policies or options; (2) a clearly defined and well-established oversight structure for the DC plan spend-down phase and providers, such as insurance companies, that offer spend down products; and (3) an approach to the spend-down phase that was different from the other countries we selected.

As part of our initial review, we interviewed and obtained comparative studies of DC systems published by academics, the Organisation for Economic

Co-operation and Development, The World Bank, and other industry experts, such as international benefits consulting firms, as well as our prior work.[6] We then examined the characteristics of each country's DC system for policies, practices, and requirements related to retirement spend-down options. On the basis of this initial review, we determined that the six countries selected could potentially provide lessons for the United States given their experience and unique approach to the spend-down phase. For each of the six countries selected, we reviewed publicly available research and reports about each country's spend-down options, oversight framework, and initiatives to educate participants about options. We also interviewed pension experts, service providers, regulatory agencies and other government officials from the countries selected. We did not conduct an independent legal analysis to verify the information provided about the laws, regulations, or policies of the foreign countries selected for this study. Instead, we relied on appropriate secondary sources, interviews with relevant officials, and other sources to support our work.

We submitted key report excerpts to agency officials in each country for their review and verification, and we incorporated their technical corrections as necessary. To provide context for various spend-down options and illustrate some of the factors that can affect retirement income we designed a retirement model and hypothetical scenarios.

To create this, we consulted with actuaries to develop a formula for pricing annuities based on benchmarks typically used by insurance companies in U.S. retail markets. We also reviewed data from the Federal Reserve Economic Database, including 10-year Treasury constant maturity rates, and Thrift Savings Plan to establish historical ranges for interest rates, inflation, and investment returns on 401(k) accounts. Appendix I provides additional information on our scope and methodology.

We conducted this performance audit from June 2012 through November 2013 in accordance with generally accepted government auditing standards. Those standards require that we plan and perform the audit to obtain sufficient, appropriate evidence to provide a reasonable basis for our findings and conclusions based on our audit objectives. We believe that the evidence obtained provides a reasonable basis for our findings and conclusions based on our audit objectives.

BACKGROUND

U.S. 401(k) Plans and Their Oversight Framework

Employers can sponsor two broad types of retirement plans, referred to in the Employee Retirement Income Security Act of 1974 (ERISA) as pension plans: (1) DB plans, which promise to provide benefits generally based on an employee's years of service and frequently are based on salary, regardless of the performance of the plans' investments, and (2) DC plans, in which benefits are based on contributions and the performance of the investments in participants' individual accounts. Since the inception of ERISA, employers have shifted away from sponsoring DB plans and moved toward sponsoring DC plans. The dominant type of DC plan is a 401(k) plan. In 2011, U.S. employers sponsored over 510,000 401(k) plans covering more than 61 million workers with more than $3.1 trillion in plan assets.[7] Unlike DB plans, in which plan participants are eligible for a specific payment for life, 401(k) plan participants typically must make their own, sometimes complex, choices about their account balance both before and during retirement. For example, participants need to decide how much to contribute, how to invest, and how to spend down savings in retirement.

In the United States, 401(k) plans are subject to provisions of ERISA, which are generally enforced by DOL's Employee Benefits Security Administration (EBSA) and Treasury's Internal Revenue Service (IRS).[8] To carry out its responsibilities under ERISA, EBSA issues regulations and other guidance. The IRS, under Title II of ERISA, and subsequent amendments to the Internal Revenue Code, generally is responsible for ensuring that plans meet certain requirements for tax qualification, among other things. Tax advantages are intended to encourage employers to establish and maintain pension plans and encourage employees to participate in the plans. For example, employer contributions to qualified plans are, within limits, tax deductible and, in general, contributions and investment earnings are not taxed as income until the employee withdraws them from the plan.

In recent years, EBSA and IRS have increased their focus on the decumulation phase of 401(k) plans, exploring ways to facilitate access to lifetime retirement income products, such as annuities. For example, in 2008, EBSA issued a new safe harbor regulation for selecting annuity providers as an optional way for sponsors and other plan fiduciaries of DC plans to satisfy their responsibilities under ERISA to act prudently and in the interest of the plan's participants and their beneficiaries.[9] Subsequently, in 2010, EBSA and

IRS sought public comments to aid the agencies in thinking about how they might facilitate access to and the use of lifetime income streams after retirement.[10] More recently, IRS proposed a new regulation in February 2012 to encourage retirement plans to offer a longevity annuity option, also referred to by some as deeply deferred annuities, in which payments initiate at an advanced age, such as age 80.[11] This regulation has not been finalized.

In addition, other entities play a role in overseeing and monitoring insurance companies that sell annuities—guaranteed income payments for life or a specified term—either through 401(k) plans or in the retail market to individual investors. For example, state insurance regulators are responsible for enforcing state insurance laws and regulations, including those covering the licensing of agents, reviewing insurance products (including annuities) and their rates, and examining insurers' financial solvency and market conduct. In addition to state insurance regulators, the National Association of Insurance Commissioners (NAIC)—a voluntary association of the heads of insurance departments from the 50 states, the District of Columbia, and five U.S. territories— plays a role in insurance regulation. Although NAIC is not a regulator, it provides guidance and services designed to more efficiently coordinate interactions between insurers and state regulators.[12] Additionally, although the Federal Insurance Office (FIO) is not directly involved in the supervision of private and public pension plans, it has a role in coordinating and developing insurance policies. FIO advises the Secretary of the Treasury on domestic and international insurance policy issues; and consults with states regarding insurance matters of national and international importance. FIO also coordinates federal efforts and develops federal policy on prudential aspects of international insurance matters. For example, FIO has been working with international regulators to develop a methodology and indicators for identifying global systemically important insurers, meaning that their failure might threaten global financial stability.

Key Aspects of DC Systems in the United States and Selected Countries

In addition to the United States, the selected countries for this review— Australia, Canada, Chile, Singapore, Switzerland, and the United Kingdom— each have extensive or growing DC retirement systems. As shown in table 1, the key features of each country's predominant DC plan vary.[13]

Table 1. Key Features of DC Plans by Country

Country	Key features of DC system	Contributions	DC assets as a percentage of national gross domestic product, 2011
Australia	Mandatory plans are known as superannuation funds, which may be established by a single employer, groups of employers in an industry, financial service companies, or even by individuals themselves.	There is a mandatory employer contribution rate of 9.25 percent of an employee's earnings, which is scheduled to gradually increase to 12 percent by 2022.	91.6%
Canada	Employers can voluntarily sponsor plans, which may be administered by a single employer, groups of employers in an industry, or financial service companies.	Contribution rates by employer and employee vary by plan. DC plans typically require employee contributions of 5 percent of earnings and matching employer contribution.	2.8
Chile	Mandatory individual retirement plans are managed by for-profit entities called Administradoras de Fondos de Pensiones (AFP).	Employers are not required to contribute to a participant's account. Employees are required to contribute 10 percent of applicable earnings and pay monthly administrative fees to their AFP.	61.3
Singapore	Mandatory plans are administered by the Central Provident Fund (CPF) Board.	For participants under age 50, employers are required to contribute 16 percent and employees 20 percent. From age 50 and older, rates gradually reduce to 6.5 percent and 5 percent for the employer and employee, respectively at age 65. Contributions are credited to accounts for retirement and for other things, such as housing and health care.	62.9

Table 1. (Continued)

Country	Key features of DC system	Contributions	DC assets as a percentage of national gross domestic product, 2011
Switzer-land	Mandatory occupational plans, which are administered by independent foundations and may be sponsored by a single employer industry associations, or insurance companies. These plans have minimum rates of returns on savings and a minimum conversion factor for annuities.[a]	Age-based contributions range from 7 percent of income for younger employees to 18 percent for employees approaching retirement. Employers are required to pay at least half of these contributions.	110.3
United Kingdom	Starting in October 2012, the United Kingdom began phasing in a requirement over 6 years that employers automatically enroll workers in a plan and make contributions to it. These plans can either be governed by a board of trustees or under a contract set up between participants and a financial service company.	In 2013, minimum contributions were 2 percent with at least 1 percent by the employer. These rates are scheduled to increase to 8 and 3 percent by October 2018, respectively.	25.2
United States	Employers can voluntarily sponsor several types of DC plans. The most popular type of DC plan is 401(k) plan. These plans are administered by employers, who may hire private companies to service the plan.	Employers, employees, or both may make contributions to the individual employee accounts.	20.9

Country	Key features of DC system	Contributions	DC assets as a percentage of national gross domestic product, 2011
		Employers may choose to make additional contributions (such as contributing a percentage of each eligible employee's salary), match the amount contributed by the employee, or both. Under IRS tax rules, contributions are limited.[b]	

Source: GAO analysis of foreign documentation, interviews with industry experts, and data from the International Monetary Fund World Economic Outlook September 2011 database. GAO did not conduct an independent legal analysis of the laws, regulations, or policies of the countries selected for this review.

[a] Officials in Switzerland said the majority of plans in Switzerland are hybrid plans. These hybrid plans are similar to cash balance plans, which in the United States are legally classified as DB plans because participants' benefits are determined by a benefit formula. However, a cash balance plan has certain features, such as notional or hypothetical "individual accounts," that make it resemble a DC plan.

[b] In the United States, the maximum annual limit for employee individual contributions to a 401(k) plan was $17,500 for 2013. The catch-up contribution limit for employees aged 50 and over was $5,500.

Retirement Spend-Down Options

At retirement, participants in DC plans enter the distribution, or spend-down phase, during which they use their savings to meet their retirement needs.[14] DC participants are typically offered one or more of three main types of spend-down options at retirement, although the availability of these options and the rules related to their use vary by country:

- **Lump sum payments** are a single distribution of some or all of a participant's retirement savings. For example, in the United States, participants generally only have the option to withdraw all or part of their account balance, which can, at the participant's discretion, then be used to invest in retail financial markets, among other things.

- **Programmed withdrawals** are a series of fixed or variable payments from a participant's account and may be administered either within a plan or in retail financial markets.[15] Programmed withdrawals attempt to produce relatively stable annual income for the lifetime of the retiree. For example, a participant could set up their own programmed withdrawal strategy and decide to draw down a certain percentage of their assets each month or year to meet their retirement needs. Governments could also set minimum and maximum drawdown limits.
- **Annuities** are guaranteed payments that are normally secured through a contract with an insurance company for either a set period or for the participant's lifetime. Annuities come in a variety of forms.[16] For example, deferred annuities allow participants to delay the start date of payments to a later point in retirement. Variable annuity payments are not guaranteed and vary based on the performance of underlying investments selected by the participant.[17]

Factors That Affect Annuity Payment Calculations Can Vary by Country

Annuity payment amounts may depend on a number of factors beyond simply the amount of retirement savings a participant can use to purchase the annuity less fees charged by insurers. These factors vary by country and may, depending on the country, include such factors as:

- Age: Participants can generally expect to receive higher payments the higher the age at which payments commence.
- Gender: Men typically receive higher payments compared to women of the same age, since studies have shown that women tend to live longer than men. This may not apply, however, in countries and market sectors that require annuities to be offered on a gender-neutral basis—such as for an annuity offered through a plan in the United States.
- Health: Participants with certain health conditions or lifestyle habits such as smoking can in some cases obtain higher payments.
- Interest rates: Participants who purchase annuities during periods of low interest rates may lock in lower payments than if they had purchased during a period of higher interest rates.

Participants face trade-offs in choosing among spend-down options because no single option protects against all the various risks participants may encounter in retirement, such as longevity[18] and inflation risk. To choose suitable options, participants approaching retirement must weigh the strengths and shortcomings of each against their own unique retirement needs. They also need to consider their other sources of retirement income, including government benefits and personal savings.[19] Table 2 illustrates some of the trade-offs participants face in choosing among spend-down options.

Table 2. Examples of Trade-offs That Participants Face in Choosing among Spend-Down Options

Spend-down option	Protects you against some risks	But may expose you to others
Lump sum payments[a]	• Provide immediate access to retirement savings, some of which can be used to pay off debt and cover the costs of unforeseen events, such as unexpected high medical costs. • Unused savings can be left as an inheritance.	• Participant is responsible for ensuring that retirement savings last their lifetime.[b] • Lump sum payments do not protect against inflation.[c] • Participant assumes investment risk for any retirement savings they reinvest.[d]
Programmed withdrawals[e]	• Enable participants to keep retirement savings invested. • Offer flexibility to choose the level and timing of payments drawn from the plan, sometimes subject to any minimum or maximum requirements. • Provide access to retirement savings to cover the costs of unforeseen events. • Unused savings can be left as an inheritance.	• Payments from programmed withdrawals are not guaranteed to last for life. • Programmed withdrawals do not protect against inflation.[c] • Participant assumes investment risk for retirement savings invested.[f]

Table 2. (Continued)

Spend-down option	Protects you against some risks	But may expose you to others
Annuities	• Provide regular payments that can be guaranteed to last the participant's lifetime.	• The decision to purchase an annuity is often irreversible. When there is an option to discontinue an annuity, it
	• Protect against investment risk, which the insurance company assumes.[g]	may subject the participant to relatively high surrender charges. • Retirement savings used to purchase an annuity cannot be left as an inheritance. • The participant risks purchasing an annuity when interest rates are low, therefore receiving lower monthly payments than expected. • Participant is at some risk of inflation unless they purchase a fully inflation indexed annuity.[h]

Source: GAO analysis.

[a] A participant who takes a lump sum payment from a plan may later, at the participant's discretion, use these assets to purchase a retail annuity or invest in retail financial markets, among other things.

[b] Depending on the tax treatment of retirement income, participants may also pay higher taxes by taking their retirement savings as a single payment in one year rather than as a series of payments spread over multiple years.

[c] In taking a lump sum payment or a programmed withdrawal, the participant is responsible for identifying and developing strategies to protect against inflation, such as purchasing an inflation protected retail annuity or achieving the investment returns necessary, net of commissions and fees, to finance increasing withdrawals.

[d] Participants can in some cases maintain preferential tax treatment on their retirement savings by rolling such savings into an individual retirement account (IRA), but as we have previously reported, the rollover process can be confusing for participants. See GAO-13-30.

[e] In the United States, there is some limited indication that plan sponsors may allow participants to set up a programmed withdrawal within a 401(k) plan. We previously found that 401(k) plans generally have lower fees and better comparative information, as well as fiduciary requirements for selecting and managing investment options relative to IRAs, see GAO-13-30.

[f] Another factor affecting the sustainability of programmed withdrawals is the sequence of investment returns—in other words, the order in which years of positive and negative investment returns occur— during the drawdown period. See GAO, Retirement Income: Ensuring Income throughout Retirement Requires Difficult Choices, GAO-11-400 (Washington, D.C.: June 7, 2011).

[g] This is not the case for variable annuities. Payments for variable annuities vary based on the performance of investments. The insurance company continues to assume the longevity risk, but the investment risk is transferred to the annuitant.

[h] Increasing payment annuities generally provide some protection against rising prices, but may not fully protect against inflation. For example, according to the Insured Retirement Institute, very few life insurance companies offer true inflation-protected annuities in the United States.

To effectively weigh the trade-offs between spend-down options, participants have to understand how interest rates, investment returns, and inflation, among other key factors, can affect their retirement income. Figure 1 below illustrates how investment returns can affect the retirement income a programmed withdrawal provides. In contrast, an annuity, once purchased, protects against investment risk over the course of retirement. Purchasing an annuity, however, may be irreversible, thereby potentially limiting the ability to leave an inheritance or cover unforeseen costs in retirement. And interest rates at the date of purchase can affect the size of payments from an annuity. In all cases, even modest inflation can erode the purchasing power of retirement income over the course of an extended retirement.

To see the effect these factors can have on retirement income from the three main spend-down options, see the interactive retirement model available at http://www.gao.gov/products/GAO-14-9.

Strategies to Improve Retirement Outcomes Have Relied on Behavioral Economics

In the last decade, some experts have emphasized an aspect of behavioral economics to help improve retirement outcomes for participants in 401(k) plans. In these plans, individuals face greater responsibility and risks in managing their retirement income needs both during the accumulation and spend-down phases, such as having insufficient savings to support a comfortable retirement and not having the right tools to make sound financial decisions about how to use what they have accumulated.[20] Our prior work found literature arguing that information or financial education, including improving financial literacy, is not necessarily the best or only approach to ensuring good retirement outcomes. They have proposed alternative strategies, sometimes in combination with information and financial education, that aim to help participants reach financial goals by making use of insights from behavioral economics—which blends economics and psychology—that indicate people are often prone to inertia and procrastination, and have difficulty processing complex information. For example, participants in 401(k) plans do not always receive timely, clear information to help them understand their options, as well as the risks and trade-offs of managing income throughout retirement. Even when such information is available, participants do not always make choices that are in their best interest. Insights from behavioral economics have led to strategies that use inertia to bolster or facilitate positive policy outcomes, such as default enrollment in 401(k) plans to increase retirement savings. Researchers and practitioners have proposed similar interventions for the spend-down phase, such as encouraging or "nudging" some participants toward annuitizing a portion of their retirement wealth.

COUNTRIES USED MULTIPLE APPROACHES TO BROADEN PARTICIPANTS' RETIREMENT OPTIONS FOR THE SPEND-DOWN PHASE

Instituting Multiple Spend-down Options Helped Participants Address Varied and Changing Risks

Although DC systems in countries we reviewed often varied in their features, structure, and regulatory oversight,[21] all six countries ensured that participants have institutionally-facilitated access to a mix of spend-down options through their plans to help them manage retirement risks.[22] Five of the six countries make the three main spend-down options—lump sum payments that offer participants flexibility to access and use their retirement savings, programmed withdrawals that allow participants to keep their account balances invested and draw on savings as needed, and annuities that offer guaranteed retirement income and protection against investment risk—explicitly available to DC participants. The countries we reviewed also allow participants to combine spend-down options to meet changing needs over the course of an extended retirement. For example, within certain conditions, participants in Singapore can take a partial lump sum after age 55 and purchase an annuity that guarantees them some amount of retirement income for life.

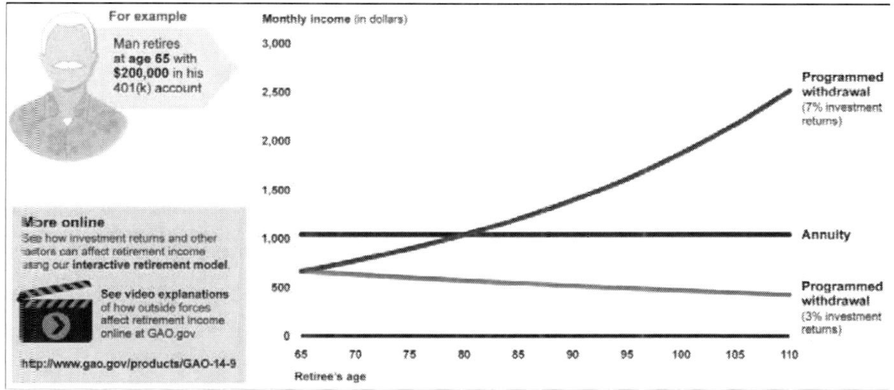

Source: GAO analysis, actuarial data on life expectancy.

Note: Annuities in this example convert 401(k) savings of $200,000—the average 401(k) plan balance for individuals in their 60s with 30 years of contributions, according to an Employee Benefit Research Institute analysis of 401(k) balances at the end of 2011—into monthly retirement income for a 65-year old male assuming interest rates of 2 percent. We selected this interest rate based on federal Thrift Savings Plan annuity rates as of May 2013. The programmed withdrawals in the figure provide monthly income totaling 4 percent of the participant's account balance each year assuming annual investment returns of either three or seven percent. These returns are in line with average 10-year historical returns on Thrift Savings Plan funds that track major U.S. stock, corporate bond, and government securities indices. There is no assurance that future investment returns will match historical returns. This example does not account for inflation, which reduces the purchasing power of retirement income. Projected monthly income does not reflect any federal income taxes on distributions from tax-deferred accounts. This example also does not account for changes in behavior in response to investment returns, such as increasing the rate of withdrawals in order to maintain a standard of living or reducing the rate of withdrawals when faced with the prospect of running out of savings.

Figure 1. Hypothetical Projection of Monthly Retirement Income for a 65-Year-Old 401(k) Plan Participant.

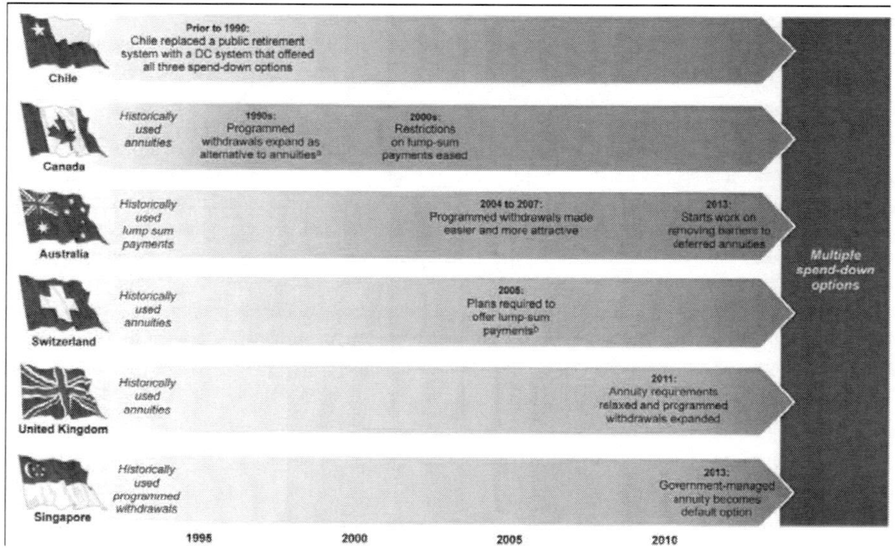

Source: GAO analysis of retirement systems in those countries; Art Explosion (flags).

Note: GAO did not conduct an independent legal analysis of the laws, regulations, or policies of the countries selected for this study.

[a] The introduction in some jurisdictions of programmed withdrawal arrangements with maximum limits on withdrawals gave participants an alternative to purchasing an annuity at retirement to meet Canada's restrictions on drawing down DC plan assets. Previously, participants could only meet these restrictions by purchasing an annuity.

[b] Switzerland does not offer programmed withdrawals as a spend-down option for participants.

Figure 2. Timeline of Key Retirement Spend-down Policy Changes in Six Countries Leading to Facilitated Access to Multiple Options for DC Plan Participants.

Other sources of retirement income, such as those from national pension systems, can address some retirement risks, but all the countries we reviewed recognize the importance of their DC system in improving retirement outcomes and have taken steps to increase participant access to multiple spend-down options. For example, Switzerland has a national pension system that provides some level of guaranteed retirement income, similar to the annuity option available to participants through their plan. Even with this system in place, in 2005 Switzerland required plans to offer participants at least 25 percent of their account balance as a lump sum payment, an option that had previously only been made at the discretion of the plan. One financial advisor we spoke with told us this policy change benefits participants who decide they already have sufficient retirement income and would accept lower annuity payments through their plan in exchange for more access to their savings at retirement.

National Pension System in Switzerland

Switzerland's national pension system has two components: an earnings-related public pension funded mainly by payroll contributions and an income-tested supplementary benefit funded by general revenues. Payment amounts for the earnings-related benefit are based on lifetime earnings. Payments in retirement are indexed to prices and earnings.

For information about the national pension systems in the other countries we reviewed, see appendix II.

Source: The World Bank and OECD.

Historically, five of the six countries tended toward one spend-down option,[23] but all have more recently expanded access to additional options, in some cases substantially altering the retirement decisions of participants, as shown in figure 2. For example, Canada had traditionally "locked in" participants' assets for the purpose of securing a stream of retirement income, which participants could previously only do by purchasing an annuity. In the 1990s, however, Canada expanded the spend-down options that would meet this locking-in requirement to include programmed withdrawals.[24] Government officials and a financial professional in Canada told us this was done in response to participants' reluctance to lose access to their assets and their desire to leave an inheritance. Programmed withdrawals have since become the most widely used spend-down option in Canada.

While each of the six countries we reviewed has multiple spend-down options to help DC plan participants tailor a retirement income strategy to fit their unique circumstances, in the United States, 401(k) plans generally only offer participants one option—a lump sum payment—leaving participants on their own to identify and develop strategies to manage retirement risks.[25] Although some 401(k) plan sponsors may offer all three of these options to participants, most do not offer annuities or programmed withdrawals similar to the systematic or formalized options[26] offered in other countries.[27] As a result, U.S. plan participants typically take a lump sum payment, and then have to make difficult choices in order for their financial assets to last throughout retirement.

Countries Undertook Reviews of the Spend-down Phase to Help Address Participants' Retirement Needs

We also found that three of the six countries conducted reviews of participants' retirement needs and concerns in the spend-down phase, which resulted in governments taking actions that led to additional spend-down options to meet those specific needs. For example, in 2007 and 2008, Singapore conducted a review of its retirement phase and determined a programmed withdrawal option designed to last approximately 20 years was not adequate to meet the needs of many participants based on their increasing longevity (see figure 3 for the key steps taken.)[28] Singapore consulted with a broad spectrum of stakeholders, including working adults, community and social sector leaders, and insurance companies and industry associations, in designing a new spend-down option to better meet participants' needs. Singapore concluded from this consultation that Singaporeans wanted an annuity scheme that provided an income for life and that would replace the programmed withdrawal option, where payouts stop completely after about 20 years. As a result, in 2009 Singapore began offering government-managed annuities, known as the Central Provident Fund Lifelong Income Scheme for the Elderly (CPF LIFE), on an opt-in basis. In 2013, Singapore set one of these CPF LIFE annuities as the default option for certain participants.

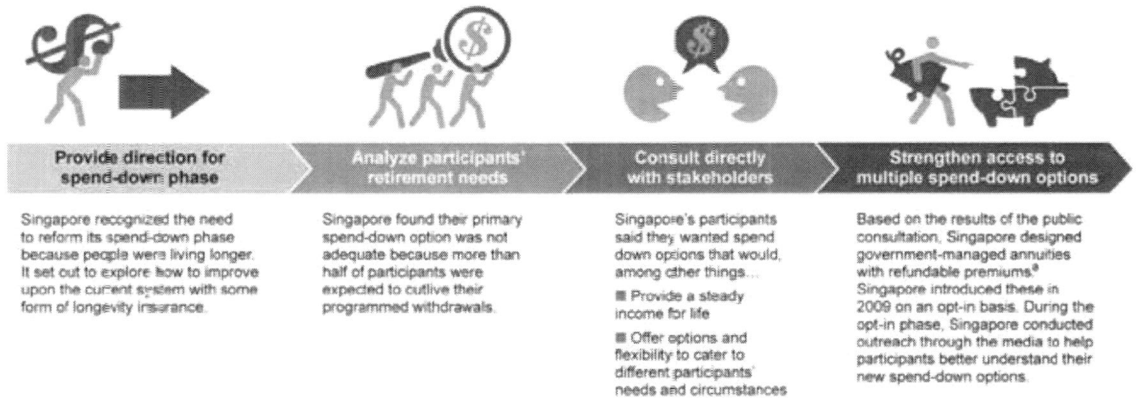

Source: GAO analysis of documents from Singapore's National Longevity Insurance Committee and Central Provident Fund.

Note: GAO did not conduct an independent legal analysis of the laws, regulations, or policies of the countries selected for this study.

[a] Participants can discontinue their annuity and get a refund of their premium less any monthly payments already made and a fee.

Figure 3. Steps Singapore Took to Strengthen Pathways to Multiple Spend-down Options.

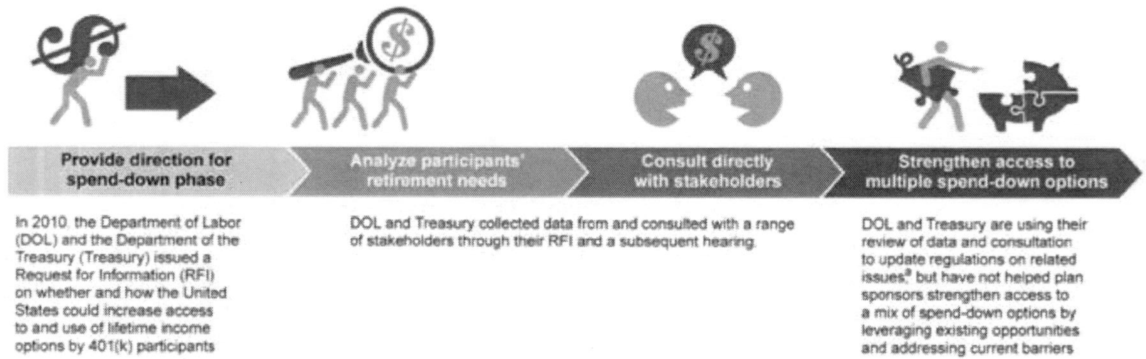

Source: GAO analysis of documents from the Department of Labor.

[a] For example, DOL is considering developing a rule that would require a participant's account balance to be expressed on his or her benefit statement as an estimated lifetime stream of payments. Pension Benefit Statements, 78 Fed. Reg. 26,727 (May 8, 2013).

Figure 4. Steps DOL and Treasury Have Taken to Explore Spend-down Options for DC Plan Participants.

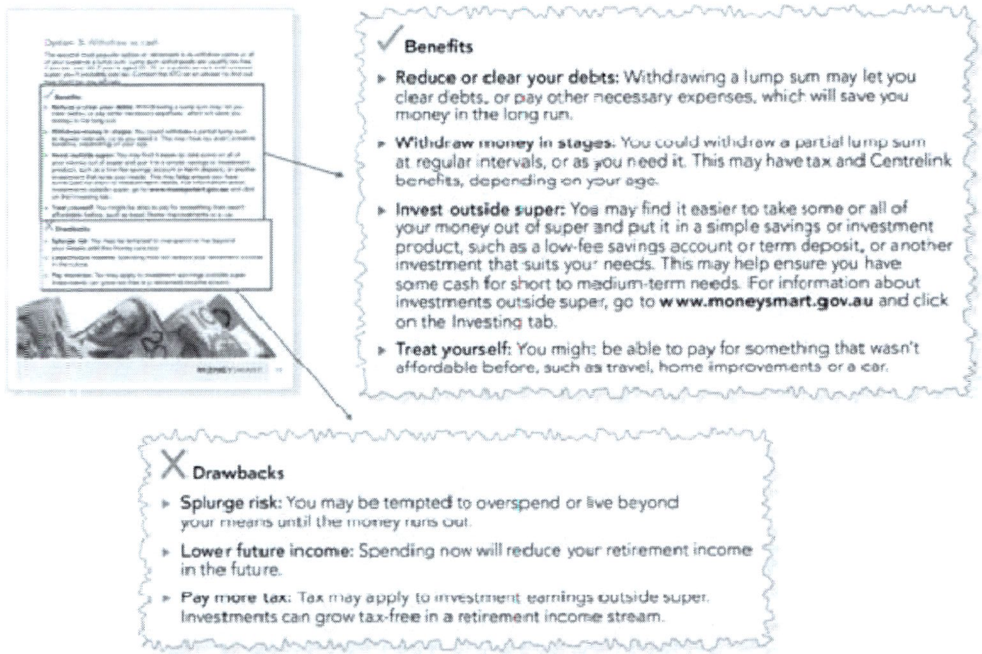

Source: GAO presentation of Australian Securities & Investments Commission information.

Figure 5. Example of Information on Spend-down Options Developed for Participants Approaching Retirement in Australia.

Similarly, the United Kingdom undertook a review to address concerns with the spend-down phase, which resulted in policy changes that provided increased flexibility for participants to choose how to spend down their account assets. Specifically, the United Kingdom determined that its long-standing rules that effectively required individuals to purchase an annuity by the age of 75 were too restrictive for an increasing number of participants—who were both living longer and working longer—and for some was acting as a barrier to saving in DC plans. As part of the review, the United Kingdom consulted with a range of stakeholders, including individuals, service providers, and industry and consumer representatives, on how to ensure that participants make appropriate spend-down choices in the absence of the annuity requirement. Based on this review, the United Kingdom removed its annuitization requirement in 2011, making this option voluntary, and expanded access to programmed withdrawals in order to give participants more flexibility to choose spend-down options that best suit them.[29] As a result, participants can remain invested in their plans and manage the timing and amount of withdrawals from their plans, within certain limitations, or delay the purchase of an annuity until interest rates are more favorable. Government officials and experts we spoke to agreed that most participants at present have not accumulated sufficient retirement savings to be eligible for and make full use of programmed withdrawals as a spend-down option.[30] According to government officials and one financial service provider, annuities remain the most widespread form of distribution from DC plans in the United Kingdom.[31] Despite current low rates of saving, the structure is in place to give workers more flexibility in planning for retirement as the DC system in the United Kingdom matures and workers accumulate larger account balances.

U.S. Regulators Have Begun to Explore the Spend-down Phase, but Have Not yet Strengthened Access to a Mix of Spend-down Options

In the United States, as shown in figure 4, similar to the steps taken by some of the other countries, DOL and Treasury have recently begun to explore the possibility of expanding 401(k) participants' access to spend-down options through their plans that offer lifetime income, but they have not yet made a concerted effort to help plan sponsors offer a mix of options to their participants. Most 401(k) plans typically only offer participants the option to take their benefits as lump sum payments, which leaves participants on their own, or to the retail market, to ensure their savings last throughout retirement. In recognition of the potential risk workers face under current conditions, DOL and Treasury undertook efforts in 2010 to collect detailed information from the public to determine what, if any, steps they could take to enhance the retirement security of 401(k) plan participants by facilitating access to, and use of, options designed to provide a stream of lifetime income after retirement.[32] Through this process, DOL and Treasury received feedback from financial service providers and other stakeholders on the challenges plan sponsors face in offering a mix of spend-down options to participants through their respective plans.[33] But the feedback also highlighted some existing flexibilities 401(k) plan sponsors have to offer multiple spend-down options. One large service provider described a range of spend-down options it offers participants, including programmed withdrawals and investment strategies that generate retirement income, such as mutual funds designed with built-in payment streams. Another service provider discussed how technology enables sponsors to offer participants access to competitive online annuity markets that can provide the benefit of competition and improved pricing at a reasonable cost.

Since 2010, DOL and Treasury have begun taking steps to improve the information participants receive about the spend-down phase and expand access to spend-down options. For example, in May 2013, DOL proposed rules that would require 401(k) participants' benefits statements to show how their account balances would translate into a stream of lifetime income payments.[34] And in February 2012, Treasury proposed rules that would make it easier to purchase deeply deferred annuities.[35] However, in contrast to the steps taken by other countries, DOL and Treasury have not yet used the information they collected to develop and implement a strategy that would help 401(k) plan sponsors leverage existing flexibilities and address challenges in offering their participants a mix of spend-down options that meet varying retirement needs. Without additional steps by U.S. regulators to help ensure sponsors are providing participants with access to a mix of options, most 401(k) plan participants are likely to continue taking a lump sum payment at retirement, regardless of whether this option is the most appropriate to meet their particular needs. By doing so, participants are at risk of either spending their assets too quickly and outliving their savings, or being too conservative with their assets, forcing them to accept a lower standard of living than necessary. Low rates of saving for retirement in the United States highlight the need to make the most of participants' 401(k) account balances. Simulations conducted by the Employee Benefit Research Institute in 2010 indicate that nearly half of workers in the United States above the age of 35 may be at risk of not having enough retirement income to meet their needs. Moreover, this problem may be more acute for those with lower incomes. When ranked by pre-retirement income, households in the lowest one-third may be at risk more than 70 percent of the time. Although all of the countries we reviewed are similarly coping with the challenge of small account balances, we found that offering a mix of options allows participants to select options that can best meet their unique circumstances.

STRATEGIES USED BY THE COUNTRIES WE STUDIED HELPED PARTICIPANTS MAKE MORE INFORMED DECISIONS

Several Approaches Used by Other Countries to Increase Participants' Knowledge and Understanding of Spend-down Options Could Help DOL's Efforts to Provide Information

Most of the countries we reviewed used various mechanisms such as communicating simple and consistent information in a timely manner to help participants make more informed spend-down decisions.[36] For example, in Australia, the government developed a booklet for participants that lays out the various spend-down options as they approach retirement with simple illustrative examples, together with the benefits and drawbacks of each, as shown in figure 5.[37] As a result, participants have access to information to plan for retirement by weighing the pros and cons of different ways to manage and make the most of their retirement savings.

Additionally, in the United Kingdom, plans are required to send a "wake up" information pack to participants 4 to 6 months before their retirement date that explains the key spend-down options, which has helped participants better understand their options.[38] The pack is also used to help plans meet the requirement to inform participants of their right to buy an annuity from a provider other than the one that holds their pension savings. In consultation with the government, the Association of British Insurers (ABI) developed a code of conduct, which requires its members—insurance companies—to communicate certain information to participants.[39] According to ABI's code of conduct, as shown in figure 6, the information in the pack should be in plain, clear language and include a cover letter detailing the participant's options and additional literature, such as a brochure on retirement facts by the U.K. government. It points participants to sources of advice and support, such as regulated advisers and independent advice organizations. In addition, the U.K. financial regulator requires that plans send participants a follow-up pack 6 to 10 weeks prior to retirement, which emphasizes the need to make a decision, among other things. ABI expects its members, who are service plan providers, to send participants communications that are in line with these practices. U.K. pension regulators told us that they also expects trust-based plan communications to meet the standards developed by the ABI, so participants in plans administered by trusts and insurance companies receive comparable information. According to a 2009 ABI study, the wake up pack increased the proportion of participants feeling quite or very comfortable about understanding their retirement options from 70 to 80 percent.[40] Their study also found that participants generally thought the information in the pack was relevant to their situations. In addition, a 2013 ABI study found that 85 percent of people who read preretirement information agreed that information from their provider made them more aware of their options at retirement.[41]

Countries we reviewed did not rely solely on the disclosure of information but also found ways to show how the information provided to participants applied to their particular circumstances. In particular, two of the six countries—Chile and the United Kingdom—help participants see how their savings would translate into a stream of retirement income by requiring plans to provide participants with monthly or yearly projections in their benefit statements, a comparison which can be useful for making retirement decisions.[42] Since 2005, Chile has required pension plans to estimate retirement income in the annual statements using multiple assumptions about the participant's expected retirement date, as shown in figure 7. For older participants about 10 years from retirement, one estimate assumes the participant stops working at the normal retirement age, while a second estimate assumes that the participant postpones retirement and continues to make contributions for 3 more years.[43] According to Chilean pension officials, the aim of these scenarios is to help participants compare their current income to expected future retirement income and to encourage them to make additional voluntary contributions in case their retirement income looks low. In fact, a 2011 study of the impact of providing these personalized pension projections to Chilean participants suggests that the receipt of this information resulted in participants making additional contributions to improve their retirement prospects.[44]

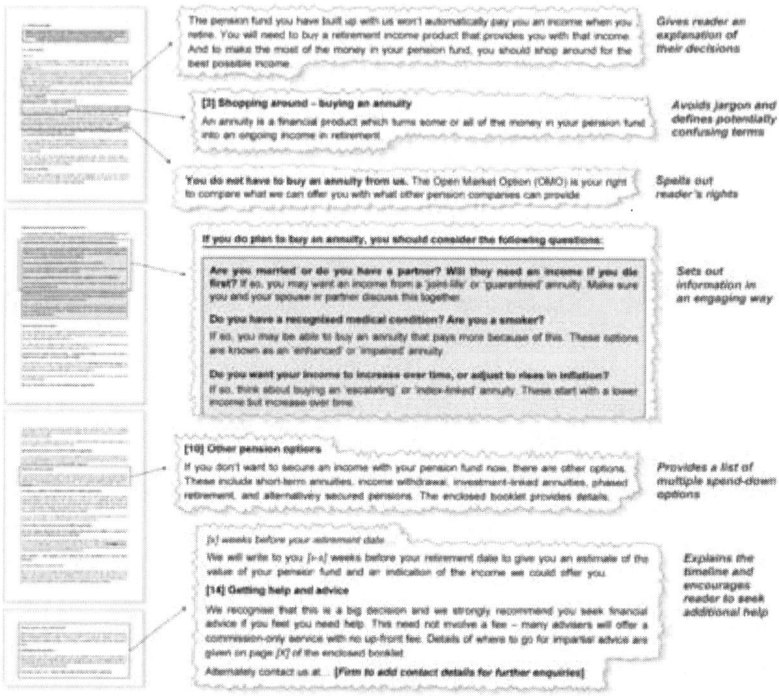

Source: GAO analysis of an Association of British Insurers (ABI) template for service providers.

Figure 6. United Kingdom Cover Letter Example of Best Practices for Communicating Spend-down Decisions and Options to Participants.

Finally, enabling participants to compare across various spend-down options and products within an option also helps them to plan for retirement. For example, we found that two of the six countries—Chile and the United Kingdom—provide electronic quotations to help near-retirees make informed decisions.

- The Chilean government introduced its central electronic quotation system (SCOMP)[45] in 2004, which lowers participant search costs and gives them easy access to transparent, reliable information by showing different spend-down options in a comparable format. The SCOMP offers individuals who are ready to retire comparable quotations for the programmed withdrawals and annuity options in a single document replacing the traditional way people looked for and bought retirement products through brokers. The SCOMP has enabled participants to more easily receive a larger amount of quality information by making all possible offers available to them without the need to hire financial intermediaries such as sales agents and brokers.[46]

- A similar benefit is available in the United Kingdom through the Money Advice Service[47] set up by the government, which allows participants to compare a range of illustrative annuity quotes on a voluntary basis. This service offers free and unbiased advice on financial matters. Specifically, Money Advice Service's website provides comparable annuity quotes from participating insurance companies, once an individual answers a set of standard questions. The individual is then presented with a table listing insurance companies and his or her annuity quotes, both in monthly, quarterly, and yearly amounts. The U.K. developed the service to provide those who do not know how to or cannot afford to get advice about annuities from other sources, particularly those with relatively small account balances. U.K. regulators told us that although participants may benefit from seeing quotes, most participants' plan balances are too small for the service to be useful for them. However, this service may become more important as more workers are automatically enrolled in plans and assets grow.[48]

In the United States, plans must provide participants certain disclosures related to their benefits and options under the plan. For example, benefit statements with the individual's account balance are required to be provided to 401(k) plan participants at least quarterly.[49] However, the disclosures do not require that participants receive information about their spend-down options before they make a decision. As a result, 401(k) plan participants may lack key information, such as the benefits and drawbacks of various spend-down options, needed to make an informed decision, and which could affect their retirement outcomes. In addition, although plan sponsors are permitted to provide information and education to participants, there is no specific guidance for sponsors to provide participants approaching retirement with information on spend-down options. Consequently, some plan sponsors may not provide participants with sufficient information, which may result in participants potentially making decisions that fail to sustain their incomes throughout retirement.

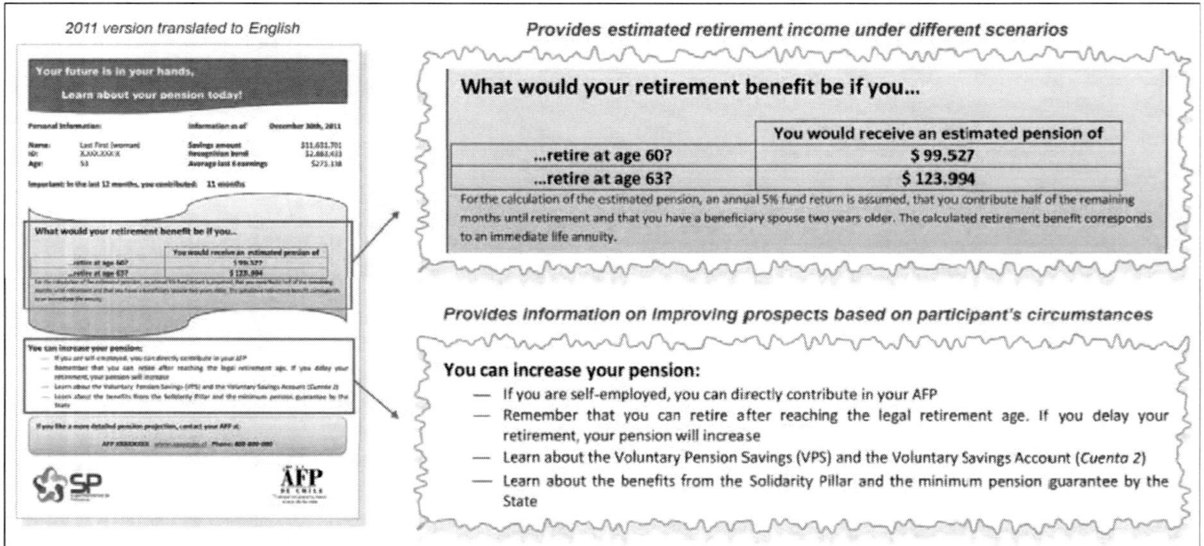

Source: Superintendence of Pensions, Chile.

Figure 7. Example of Chile's Benefit Statement Illustrating Projected Income.

DOL has begun to consider including lifetime income projections in benefit statements, which may yield positive outcomes for participants. Currently, 401(k) plan benefit statements generally only show a participant's account balance, and according to DOL officials participants may have difficulty predicting how long their savings will last. An April 2013 study funded by DOL found that more than half of a sample of plan statements did not include projections of the participant's balance at retirement, estimates of the retirement income they might be able to expect at retirement, or the "relationship between future outcomes and current savings or investment behavior."[50] In May 2013, DOL announced that it was considering developing proposed regulations regarding DC plan benefit statements, and solicited public comments to inform its thinking as it considers possible regulatory proposals.[51] One idea is to show a participant's current account balance and an estimated lifetime stream of payments based on such balance, assuming the participant is at normal retirement age as of the date of the statement, even if he or she is younger. The second idea is aimed at participants who have not yet reached normal retirement age, which shows a projected account balance at normal retirement age and then converts to an estimated lifetime stream of payments. As shown in Chile, including lifetime income projections on plan statements, similar to those being considered by DOL, can help participants envision and understand the lifetime monthly income that can be generated from an account balance.

Most of the Countries We Reviewed Use Incentives to Encourage Certain Kinds of Participant Behavior

Recognizing that disclosure of information alone is not always sufficient to ensure good retirement outcomes, several countries also use subtle incentives or nudges to promote particular kinds of behavior. In particular, two countries we reviewed—Singapore and Switzerland—use defaults to exploit inertia and promote a specific option.[52] In Switzerland, for example, some plans use annuities as the default spend-down option allowing for the possibility of opting out. One study suggests the take-up rate of annuities is higher in such plans relative to those where the lump sum option is the default.[53] In contrast, the United Kingdom is attempting to address participants' inertia in shopping for annuities. Until recently, most participants purchased an annuity from their existing service provider, partly because the wake up pack they received shortly before retiring included an application for an annuity with that provider, although it might not have offered the best rate. Working together, the U.K. government and ABI agreed that to promote the search for better annuity rates providers should not include an annuity application in the pack.[54]

In addition, tax incentives are also used to encourage or deter the use of certain spend-down options. For example, in 2007, the Australian government removed the favorable tax treatment enjoyed by annuities, which caused the relatively small market for life annuities to virtually disappear, and negatively affected the market for term annuities as well, according to researchers. In addition, researchers found that a series of reforms between 2005 and 2007 contributed to the rapid increase in the demand for programmed withdrawals.[55] For example, the reforms exempted from taxes all earnings or investment returns on assets kept in superannuation funds to support programmed withdrawals, provided that minimum age-based annual drawdowns are satisfied. A report by the Australian pension regulators showed an increase in the proportion of retirement income taken as programmed withdrawals from one third in 2005 to one half by 2012.[56] Over the same period, the proportion of superannuation funds offering programmed withdrawals increased from 35 percent to 80 percent.

Countries Also Assist Participants Who Rely on Financial Advisors

Three of the countries we reviewed implemented policies to strengthen safeguards regarding financial advisors, so that DC plan participants seeking professional advice have the opportunity to receive fair and objective information that enables them to better manage their retirement income. These countries recognized that spend-down decisions can be complex for participants, who may choose to rely on the assistance of a financial advisor to help make appropriate choices. As a result, countries such as the United Kingdom have taken steps to protect DC participants against inappropriate fees and unscrupulous advice in making spend-down decisions. For example, since January 1, 2013, financial advisors in the United Kingdom are prohibited from receiving commissions on products they sell in order to reduce the sale of costly and unfit products and minimize conflicts of interest. Instead, they now have to explain to participants how much advice will cost and reach agreement with the participant on a price and method of payment, such as an upfront fee or installments. Since 2008, Chile requires that those who previously worked as annuity brokers broaden their knowledge to all aspects of pensions before being registered as advisors. This knowledge enables them to provide participants and their beneficiaries with comprehensive information needed to make informed decisions about their benefits based on their needs and interests.

Countries' Regulation and Oversight of Spend-down Options Offer Lessons for U.S. Regulators

Most of the Countries We Reviewed Used Withdrawal Rules to Help Protect Participants from Outliving Their Savings

Most of the countries we reviewed imposed income requirements or withdrawal limits on lump sum payments to help those who take this option mitigate retirement risks.[57] For example, in three of the six countries, participants must meet retirement income requirements if they wish to withdraw all or part of their DC plan assets as a lump sum. Specifically, in order for participants in Chile to be eligible to access part of their account, they would need to accumulate enough income to finance 100 percent of the maximum pension with a government supplement and a 70 percent or higher replacement rate based on the last 10 years of their salaries.[58] According to the Chilean pensions regulator, participants who meet these conditions can withdraw any amount in excess of the amount needed to meet the minimum.[59] Under these rules, relatively few participants have taken partial lump sum payments and, of those who did, the amounts were generally quite small. In contrast, Australia does not place an upper limit on the amount participants can withdraw as a lump sum. According to researchers and government officials, participants in Australia who choose this option may run the risk of outliving their savings and becoming solely reliant on government benefits for retirement income. However, some researchers and government officials we spoke with said retirees in Australia may actually be overly cautious in spending down their assets and face the opposite risk of accepting a lower standard of living than is necessary to meet their retirement needs. In the United States, lump sum distributions from 401(k) plans are subject to few restrictions. During our 2011 review of the choices retirees make in managing their assets, we found that some U.S. plan participants prefer to have access to their full 401(k) plan retirement savings, such as by rolling their assets over into an individual retirement account (IRA) or withdrawing them when they retire. At retirement, 401(k) plan participants may withdraw their full account balance as a lump sum and may be required to pay federal and state income taxes on that amount.[60]

Of the five countries that offer programmed withdrawals, four countries regulate them to help prevent participants from spending their savings too quickly. For example, Chile's 2008 pension reforms introduced an additional actuarial factor in the government calculation of the maximum withdrawal amount to account for longevity risks. The maximum withdrawal amount is calculated so payments do not drop below a certain floor, 30 percent of the first payment, by the time participants reaches the age of 98. As a result of these reforms, a retiree's benefits can vary year to year based on life expectancy estimates and projected returns on investments, but will not fall below a certain amount.[61] Canada also limits the annual amount a participant can withdraw from programmed withdrawal products. Regulators in some Canadian jurisdictions impose an annual maximum withdrawal, which helps to ensure participants have a regular income up to age 90.

Most 401(k) plan participants in the United States do not have access to programmed withdrawal products through their plans similar to the ones we found in other countries. The primary programmed withdrawal option that U.S. plan participants may be aware of is the required minimum distributions in tax-deferred plans, such as 401(k) plans, when a participant reaches 70 ½.[62] If a plan offers a systematic withdrawal and the participant designs and manages their programmed withdrawal, the extent to which their strategy is successful at providing income throughout retirement depends on a number of factors, such as the rate of drawdown, future investment returns, inflation, and longevity. For an illustration about how some of these factors may affect retirement income, see the additional materials at http://www.gao.gov/products/GAO-14-9.

DOL Continues to Look at Barriers Plan Sponsors Face in Offering Annuities to 401(k) Plan Participants, Which Do Not Exist in the Countries We Reviewed

DOL is in the process of reviewing regulatory barriers that may prevent or discourage 401(k) plan sponsors from offering annuities to participants. In the United States, 401(k) plan sponsors who offer an annuity to their participants through their plan are subject to fiduciary standards in their selection of an annuity provider, which require them to act solely in the interest of the plan's participants and their beneficiaries. In 2008, DOL issued new final regulations, in the form of a safe harbor, for the selection of annuity providers to help plans prudently choose them and to some extent encourage plans to offer annuities.[63] In proposing the safe harbor DOL speculated that an annuity option would give more participants the opportunity to annuitize their savings, while not impeding them from choosing other options.[64] Even with this safe harbor, according to some U.S. retirement experts and plan service providers, sponsors of 401(k) plans may be hesitant to offer an annuity to their participants because of the additional burden and the potential liability sponsors may incur. In 2010, some respondents to DOL's request for information on lifetime income options, which included some questions related to the existing safe harbor provision, suggested that DOL revise one condition of the safe harbor that requires sponsors to assess the ability of an insurance company to make all future payments under an annuity contract. Respondents in favor of DOL revising the condition noted that it could help ease some DC plan sponsors' concerns about offering an annuity as a spend-down option. Additionally, this could help participants who would otherwise purchase an annuity in the retail market gain access to group prices, which are typically lower than individual prices.[65] In December 2012, the ERISA Advisory Council reported on the importance to the retirement community that DOL develop guidance designed to provide meaningful assistance to plan sponsors and participants by modifying the existing safe harbor provision that governs the selection of an annuity provider. In its report, the ERISA Advisory Council also encouraged DOL to partner with NAIC to help with its effort to develop a more workable safe harbor for the selection of annuities and other lifetime income products.[66] In 2012, DOL began working with the NAIC ERISA Retirement Income Working Group as they consider possible options for easing plan sponsor concerns with the financial soundness of annuity providers as related to the DOL safe harbor for the selection of an annuity provider and fiduciary responsibilities.

In the countries we reviewed, employers are not expected to assess an annuity provider's ability to make future payments before contracting with them to offer an annuity through their plans. According to regulators in each of the countries we reviewed, there are no requirements for employers to assess the financial stability of an insurer and countries generally rely on insurance regulations and industry standards to oversee and monitor insurance companies, including those that sell annuities.[67]

For example, in Canada, regulators told us that insurers must meet solvency requirements[68] and financial market conduct standards, and all insurers are members of an association that promotes consistent insurance practices and standards by issuing guidelines to its members. Moreover, in four of the six countries regulators and industry practitioners told us that the main responsibility of employers is to contribute to the plan during accumulation, and their obligations typically cease at retirement.[69] In the United Kingdom, where plans are required to inform participants of their right to shop around for an annuity, there are no requirements to assess the potential annuity provider the participant may select through the plan. According to U.K. government officials, plan trustees and participants do not have the expertise to assess the solvency of an annuity provider and are not expected to do so. Furthermore, they noted that this responsibility lies with the bank and insurance company regulators, so plans offering and participants purchasing an annuity are assured of the provider's solvency. Additionally, because plans do not need to take steps to assess annuity providers, there are no additional administrative costs associated with offering an annuity through the plan. As some of the countries we reviewed illustrate, the absence of a requirement for plan sponsors to assess annuity providers allows plans to more easily provide participants a way to annuitize their retirement savings, if they so choose.

CONCLUSION

The DC systems in the countries we reviewed differ from the United States in a number of ways, and not all the lessons they have to offer would apply here, but their experiences illustrate additional steps DOL and Treasury could consider to help 401(k) plan sponsors make the most of existing flexibilities to offer multiple spend-down options through their plan and broaden participants' retirement options. By 2015, participants whose retirement savings will be primarily made up of what they accumulated in their 401(k) plans will either be eligible to retire or approaching retirement and many will be faced with the challenge of ensuring they do not outlive their retirement savings. Yet, most of these participants' 401(k) plans will offer lump sum payments as the primary spend-down option for participants, leaving them to their own devices to figure out how to make their savings meet their needs and last throughout their retirement. Some participants may prefer having complete access to their retirement savings upon retirement. Others, however, could benefit from knowing that there are options offered through the plan—other than a lump sum payment—that might be optimal for them. The experiences of other countries have shown that participants benefit from being able to select among multiple, competitively priced and easily accessible options to address their diverse and changing retirement needs. Although DOL and Treasury have taken some initial steps to explore how the United States might expand the options available to 401(k) participants at retirement, they could do more to ensure that plan sponsors offer flexible options to participants, enabling them to choose the spend-down option that best fits their particular circumstances.

Our work also shows that information provided in an easy to understand format at appropriate times before a participant retires can help participants think about and plan for the amount they will need on a monthly basis during retirement. Receiving information on projected income with their account statements helps workers develop and focus on retirement income targets, which in turn can lead to positive changes in participant behavior, such as working longer to improve their prospects for a successful retirement. Comparing available spend-down options and longevity risk can also help participants understand the advantages and disadvantages of each option available to them. In addition, as illustrated in our interactive retirement model, learning to understand the effects of interest rates, inflation, and returns on each type of spend-down option can help participants begin to interpret financial information that can impact their retirement income. Given that DOL is considering various approaches to improve 401(k) plan participants' understanding of retirement income, it is clear that including information about spend-down options and estimated income can further help participants make more sound decisions about their retirement income.

Finally, unlike within 401(k) plans in the United States, in the countries we reviewed annuities were generally an option available to participants through their plans. Because few 401(k) plans in the United States choose to offer annuities to participants, they may be missing a beneficial spend-down option that can provide lifetime income at discounted group prices. As DOL continues to look at the barriers to 401(k) plans offering annuities, the lack of requirements for plan sponsors in other countries to assess an annuity provider's ability to make future payments—relying instead on the adequacy of insurance regulation—may be something to explore. Our work shows that offering annuities to participants can be done in an easy cost-effective manner enabling participants, if they prefer to consider this spend-down option and not dismiss it as being too expensive to obtain.

Recommendations for Executive Action

As DOL and Treasury continue their efforts to determine the actions needed to enhance the retirement security of 401(k) plan participants, we recommend they consider the approaches taken by other countries to formalize access to multiple spend-down options for U.S. plan participants that address varying retirement risks and needs. To the extent possible, lessons from other countries should be used to help DOL and Treasury ensure plan sponsors have information about their flexibilities and the ability to facilitate access to a mix of appropriate options for 401(k) plan participants.

In addition, as DOL considers changes to participant benefit statements and other disclosures, we recommend that the Secretary of DOL consider strategies other countries have employed to help participants make sound decisions, such as providing timely information at or before retirement about available spend-down options and projections of future retirement income.

We also recommend that as DOL continues to review regulatory barriers to lifetime income options for 401(k) plan participants it consider other countries' approaches to plans offering annuities, such as their reliance on existing solvency requirements and insurance industry standards to provide assurances rather than place responsibility on plan sponsors to make an assessment of an annuity provider's financial stability. As DOL considers the approaches of other countries and continues to work with NAIC, which facilitates interactions between insurance companies and state insurance regulators, DOL may wish to consult with the Federal Insurance Office, which coordinates federal efforts on prudential aspects of international insurance matters.

Agency Comments and Our Evaluation

We provided a draft of this report to DOL and Treasury for comment. Both agencies provided technical comments that were incorporated, as appropriate. In its written response, DOL generally agreed with our recommendations and stated that it will take steps to address these recommendations in its ongoing efforts. Moreover, DOL will be focusing on two areas for further consideration that we highlighted in our report, participant education and providing regulatory assistance to plan sponsors considering an annuity option in defined contribution plans.

Regarding our recommendation that DOL and Treasury consider the approaches of other countries to formalize access to multiple spend-down options for 401(k) plan participants, DOL commented that expanding access to additional options involves plan design features, which historically have not been subject to DOL's regulatory authority under Title I of ERISA. DOL noted that it will evaluate whether there are available regulatory approaches to address this recommendation. As we addressed in the report, participants can benefit from having access to a mix of options allows participants to select options that can best meet their unique circumstances. Therefore, we support DOL's efforts to look into available regulatory approaches to address our recommendation and would encourage the agency to fully consider the steps it could take within the scope of its current authority.

With respect to our recommendation to consider the strategies of other countries to help participants make sound retirement decisions, DOL agreed that participants should have timely information at or before retirement about available spend-down options and projections of future retirement income and stated that they will explore their options for actions. As we illustrated in our report, having timely information and projections of future income can help plan participants make more informed retirement saving decisions. We would again encourage DOL to fully consider what steps it could take within the scope of its current authority.

Finally, with respect to our third recommendation that DOL consider other countries' approaches as it reviews regulatory barriers to lifetime income options to 401(k) plan participants, DOL stated that it will evaluate the available regulatory approaches to address our recommendation. We also suggested that DOL consult with NAIC and FIO in its efforts. DOL commented that it began working with a NAIC Working Group to consider possible options for easing plan sponsor concerns with the financial soundness of annuity providers in connection with DOL's safe harbor for the selection of annuity providers and fiduciary responsibilities. DOL noted that the NAIC Working Group plans on providing EBSA with a list of "best practices" for fiduciaries when asking states for information about insurers, and that it will continue to work with NAIC, Treasury, FIO, and others as it evaluates regulatory approaches to address our recommendation. In response to DOL's comment, we revised our draft to reflect the status of DOL's efforts to collaborate with NAIC on the safe harbor for the selection of annuity providers. We commend DOL for its initiative to develop a more workable safe harbor, but continue to encourage DOL to review alternative approaches taken by other countries, such as their reliance on existing solvency requirements and insurance standards. As shown in our report, these approaches can ease the burden on plan sponsors. As a result of DOL's review and potential action, 401(k) plans could more easily offer annuities to plan participants, which allow them greater flexibility to choose spend-down options that meet their needs and preferences.

Charles A. Jeszeck, Director
Education, Workforce, and Income Security Issues

APPENDIX I. OBJECTIVES, SCOPE, AND METHODOLOGY

Our objectives for this review were to examine selected countries' (1) approaches to offering retirement spend-down options; (2) key strategies to help participants make sound decisions; and (3) approaches to regulating and overseeing options.

To address these objectives, we conducted in-depth reviews of retirement spend-down phase strategies in countries with extensive or growing defined contribution (DC) systems to determine lessons for the United States based on best practices used in other countries. We selected the following countries for this review: Australia, Canada, Chile, Singapore, Switzerland, and the United Kingdom (U.K.). In selecting the six countries, we considered if the country had (1) developed innovative spend-down phase policies or options; (2) a clearly defined and well-established oversight structure for the DC plan spend-down phase and providers, such as insurance companies; and (3) if the country's approach to the spend-down phase was uniquely different from the other countries in our scope. To determine which countries to include, we conducted an initial review of the universe of countries with well-developed account based retirement systems. We reviewed comparative studies of DC systems published by GAO, academics, the Organisation for Economic Co-operation and Development (OECD), The World Bank, and other industry experts, such as international benefits consulting firms, to determine which countries have extensive or growing DC systems and if those countries had developed innovative spend-down policies or options. We solicited recommendations on countries with innovative spend-down phase approaches or options from representatives of the OECD, The World Bank, U.S. government officials, academics, and industry practitioners who work with multi-national companies that operate in other countries with DC plans. We then examined the characteristics of each country's DC system for policies, practices, and requirements related to retirement spend-down options. Based on our initial review, we excluded countries in which the DC plan is structured in a substantially different manner from that of U.S. 401(k) plans or not well-developed relative to other pension options, or in which the spend-down phase was not well-defined. We also determined that the six countries selected could potentially provide lessons for the United States given their experience and unique approach to the spend-down phase.

For each of the six countries we selected, we reviewed publicly available research and reports about each country's pension systems—particularly information on spend-down options, oversight framework, and initiatives to educate participants about options. We also interviewed pension experts, service providers, regulatory agencies and other government officials from the countries selected. We did not conduct an independent legal analysis to verify the information provided about the laws, regulations, or policies of the countries selected for this study. Instead, we relied on appropriate secondary sources, interviews with relevant officials, and other sources to support our work. We submitted key report excerpts to agency officials in each country for their review and verification, and we incorporated their technical corrections as necessary.

In addition to addressing these objectives, we also developed a retirement model to help provide contextual information on spend-down options and certain factors that may affect retirement income from these options. The retirement model to allow users to view retirement income under a range of circumstances provided by three main spend-down options: (1) a lump sum payment of their account balance; (2) a programmed withdrawal with payments that are either fixed or set as a proportion of the remaining account balance; and (3) an immediate annuity that makes level payments with no joint or survivor benefit. We developed, in consultation with GAO's Chief Actuary and an external actuary with expertise in annuity pricing, a formula that was calibrated to approximate annuity payments similar to those found in U.S. retail annuity markets in July, 2013.[70] We simulated retail annuity prices because participants in most 401(k) plans do not have access to institutionally priced annuities within plans. For instance, to purchase an annuity, these participants would instead have to roll over a lump sum payment of their account balance into an IRA and purchase an annuity as an individual investor in U.S. retail markets. To set the ranges within which users can adjust assumptions about interest rates, investment returns and inflation, we analyzed historical data on economic indicators from the Federal Reserve Economic Database, including 10-year Treasury constant maturity rates, and investment returns from Thrift Savings Plan funds that track broad stock, fixed income, and government securities indices. To ensure the annuity rates generated from our model reflected U.S. retail market rates as of July 31, 2013, we calibrated rates using quotes from ImmediateAnnuities.com. We did not assess the reliability of data used to set ranges or calibrate rates, mainly because the information generated from the interactive tool provides illustrative context for the report and is not material to findings, conclusions, or recommendations. In addition, retirement income depicted in the interactive tool does not reflect any federal income taxes on distributions from tax-deferred 401(k) accounts.[71] Dollar amounts in the interactive tool are for illustrative purposes only and should not be considered as quotes for spend-down products or taken as financial advice.

We conducted this performance audit from June 2012 to November 2013 in accordance with generally accepted government auditing standards. Those standards require that we plan and perform the audit to obtain sufficient, appropriate evidence to provide a reasonable basis for our findings and conclusions based on our audit objectives. We believe that the evidence obtained provides a reasonable basis for our findings and conclusions based on our audit objectives.

APPENDIX II. KEY FEATURES OF DC PENSION SYSTEMS IN AUSTRALIA, CANADA, CHILE, SINGAPORE, SWITZERLAND, AND THE UNITED KINGDOM

Australia

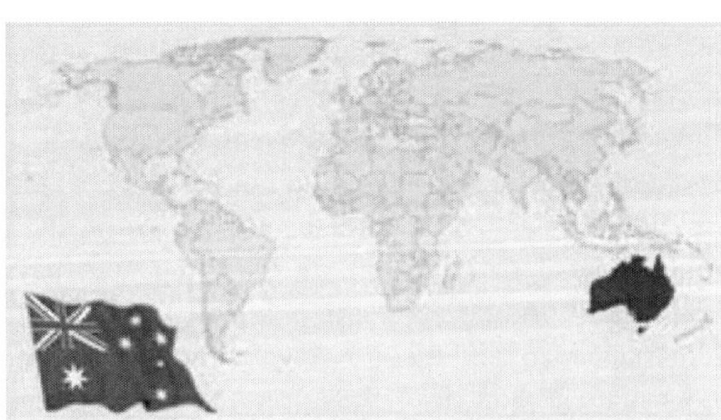

At a glance

Since 1992, Australia has had a mandatory defined contribution (DC) pension system, known as the superannuation guarantee.[72] Employees generally designate a plan, known as a superannuation fund, to which the employer is required to direct contributions. Employees who do not designate a fund are placed in a default accumulation option, known from 2013 as MySuper. In 2010, Australia announced plans to gradually increase mandatory contributions from 9 to 12 percent of workers' wages by 2022. The average account balance at normal retirement age is about AUD 119,000 (approximately *$110,000*) as of 2012.

- **Total system assets:** AUD 1.4 trillion (*$1.3 trillion*) as of 2012
- **Percentage of workers with DC accounts:** not available during our review

Types of plans

Industry funds are generally non-profit entities[73] established by a single employer or group of employers. Industry funds generally offer 5 to 15 investment options designed to meet most participants' needs and in recent years many have become available to the public rather than being restricted to the employees of particular employers.

Corporate funds are set up by an employer for their employees, although many meet their obligations by contributing to industry or retail funds on behalf of their employees

Retail funds are for-profit entities usually run by banks or investment companies. They often have a large number of mid to higher priced investment options and are open to anyone.

Self-managed superannuation funds are available to individuals who create and manage their own plan, which entails establishing a trust and a bank account. Up to four people can be in a self-managed fund, however each individual must be a trustee or director of the trustee company and no "arms-length" employees are permitted, according to APRA officials.

Source: GAO analysis of foreign agency documents and interviews with Australian officials and industry experts; State Department (base map); Art Explosion (flags)

Note: GAO did not conduct an independent legal analysis of the laws, regulations, or policies of the countries selected for this review

DC Spend-Down Options

- **Lump sums:** Participants may take some or all of their account balance as a lump sum payment.
- **Programmed withdrawals:** Participants have the flexibility to structure the timing and amount of withdrawals subject only to annual required minimum withdrawals. These options are known as account-based income streams or account-based pensions.
- **Annuities:** Only a small number of annuities are purchased annually, and most are term annuities that provide payments over a fixed period rather than lifetime annuities that guarantee payments for the participant's life.

Providers

Spend-down options may be provided by employers or a group of employers, banks, insurance companies, or financial service providers.

Regulators

- **The Australian Prudential Regulatory Authority** (APRA) is responsible for prudential regulation of all superannuation funds except for self-managed superannuation funds and some public sector schemes. Reforms implemented in July 2013 will enhance APRA's ability to set and enforce prudential standards. According to officials, APRA's authority prior to this had largely been limited to issuing, setting conditions on, and revoking licenses to operate superannuation funds. APRA is also responsible for the prudential regulation of other financial services entities, such as banks and insurance companies.
- **The Australian Securities and Investments Commission** licenses and monitors financial services businesses to ensure they operate efficiently, honestly, and fairly. This includes superannuation trustees who hold a license with the commission. It also operates a website that provides consumers information to help them make smart choices about their personal finances, including spend-down decisions, www.moneysmart.gov.au.
- **The Australian Taxation Office** is responsible for regulating self-managed superannuation funds, which it does by providing information to trustees on how to set up and manage their fund, checking that the fund complies with standards and laws, and taking enforcement actions to correct breaches of the law.

National Pension System

Australia's Age Pension is a pay-as-you-go public pension funded out of general revenues. The Age Pension is designed to provide biweekly retirement income equal to about 28 percent of average wages,[74] as well as other benefits such as assistance for health care and transportation, to residents of Australia age 65 and older.[75] The Age Pension is means tested for both income and assets, so accumulations in superannuation will reduce biweekly payments from the Age Pension. According to APRA officials, the Age Pension is essentially a "safety-net" provided for those unable to provide for themselves.

Canada

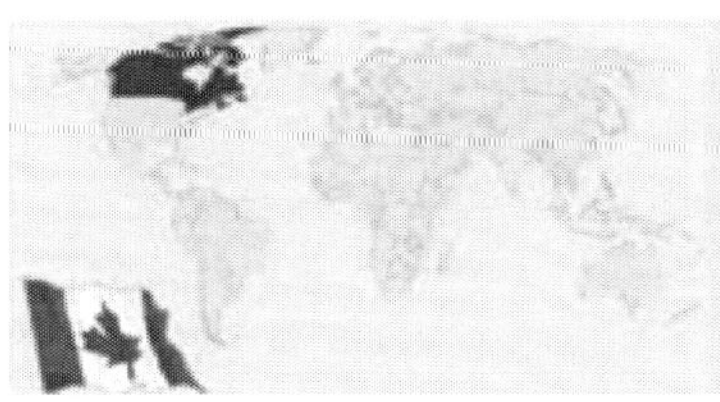

At a glance

Although, most private voluntary occupational pension plans have been DB, almost all new plans are DC, and a typical DC plan would require employee contributions of 5 percent of earnings and matching employer contribution.

- **Total system assets:**
  47.42 billion Canadian dollars (*about $45.16 billion*) as of 2011
- **Percentage of workers with DC accounts:**
  5 percent as of 2011

Types of plans

Voluntary private plans are known as registered private pension plans and can either be DC plans or DB plans. In general, money payable to a member of a plan can only be used to provide retirement income, even if a member leaves the plan. Once benefits are vested, they are usually "locked-in," which helps to ensure that a member will have regular income at retirement, and creditors cannot seize locked-in pension benefits.

Source: GAO analysis of foreign agency documents and interviews with Australian officials and industry experts; State Department (base map); Art Explosion (flags).

Note: GAO did not conduct an independent legal analysis of the laws, regulations, or policies of the countries selected for this review.

Highlights of the Spend-Down Phase

DC Spend-Down Options

- **Lump sums:** Partial lump sums may be available under certain conditions. These conditions vary by jurisdiction.
- **Programmed withdrawals:** Registered income funds and life income funds are available to participants, depending on the jurisdiction. Minimum distribution requirements, beginning at age 71, apply to these products. In addition, where life income funds are available, participants' accounts may be subject to maximum distribution requirements, set as fixed percentages of account balances, at each age, designed to last up to a certain age. In a few jurisdictions, regulators have allowed plans to offer a type of programmed withdrawal, known as a variable benefit. Instead of transferring a participant's balance to a third party, assets remain in the plan and are distributed by the plan.
- **Annuities:** An array of other life annuities is available in the retail market. The most common form is a single life pension with a minimum guarantee of 5 or 10 years of payments. A plan administrator must purchase an annuity for a participant of a DC plan if the member does not elect to exercise of their options. According to regulators, the take-up rate for annuities is relatively low.

Providers

Programmed withdrawal products are generally offered by financial institutions, such as banks and trustee companies. Private insurance companies offer annuities.

Regulators

Plans are generally regulated at the provincial level, so policies vary by province and the federal level. At the federal level, the Office of the Superintendent of Financial Institutions regulates and supervises private pension plans in federally regulated areas of employment, such as banking, telecommunications and inter-provincial transportation. It is also the regulator for pension plans established with respect to employment in the Yukon, the Northwest Territories, and Nunavut.

National Pension System

Canada has a two-tier social security system that provides the majority of retirement income for the average worker. The system includes the Old Age Security program, which provides monthly payment to residents who are 65 years of age and over as well as a guaranteed income supplement—a family income-tested benefit—to low-income pensioners; and the Canada Pension Plan, which pays a monthly retirement pension to people who have worked and contributed to the Canada Pension Plan.[76] The amount of the Canada Pension Plan benefit a person is entitled to depends on how much and for how long that person contributed to the plan.

Chile

At a glance

Chile instituted a DC pension system in 1981. Workers who entered the labor market after that date are mandated to contribute to an individual DC account.

- **Total system assets:** 77.5 trillion Chilean pesos (*about $162 billion*)as of 2012
- **Percentage of workers with DC accounts:** About 59 percent of those in the labor force currently contribute as of 2012

Types of plans

Workers are free to choose a licensed for-profit service provider, known as an AFP (Administradoras de Fondos de Pensiones) to manage their individual accounts. Currently, there are six AFPs.

New entrants to the labor force are defaulted to the AFP with the lowest fee as determined by a bidding process, which takes place every 2 years.They are required to remain in this AFP for 2 years, after which they can freely choose a service provider.

Source: GAO analysis of foreign agency documents and interviews with Australian officials and industry experts; State Department (base map); Art Explosion (flags).

Note: GAO did not conduct an independent legal analysis of the laws, regulations, or policies of the countries selected for this review.

Highlights of the Spend-Down Phase

DC Spend-Down Options

- **Lump sums:** Participants may take some of their account balance as a lump sum payment provided the remaining balance is enough to generate a pension equal to 100 percent of the maximum pension with solidarity support, 261,758 Chilean pesos (about $520) monthly as of December 2012, and 70 percent of the participant's average monthly taxable wage for the previous 10 years.
- **Programmed withdrawals:** AFPs administer this option with the monthly amount determined annually by a government formula based on account balance, expected rate of return, inflation, and gender-specific life expectancy.
- **Annuities:** Administered by life insurance companies, the annuity calculation is based on age and gender-specific life expectancy. Participants can combine options such as temporary programmed withdrawals with a deferred annuity, or purchase an immediate annuity with a portion of their account balance and programmed withdrawals with the rest. Annuities are inflation-indexed. Annuities are not allowed if the pension they generate is smaller than the Basic Solidarity pension, which as of December 2012 was 80,528 Chilean pesos (about $160) monthly.

Providers

- AFPs administer programmed withdrawals. Insurance companies offer annuities to participants.

Regulators

- **The Superintendent of Pensions** closely supervises and regulates AFPs, including issuing licenses for them to participate in the system. On an ongoing basis, the Superintendent of Pensions monitors plan providers for compliance with investment option guidelines, reserve requirements, fee structure, and other requirements.
- **The Superintendent of Securities and Insurance** supervises insurance companies, which includes setting rules and regulations about solvency principles and monitoring insurance company offers through the SCOMP system.[77] Together with the Superintendent of Pensions, it maintains a list of approved pension advisors.

National Pension System

Chile has a public pension system with two components targeted at the poorest 60 percent of the population age 65 and over who meet residency requirements. There is a Basic Solidarity Pension for individuals who have not contributed to individual accounts and pass the means test. Participants who contributed to individual accounts and pass the means test receive a Pension Solidarity Complement if their monthly pension is below a threshold amount of 261,758 Chilean pesos (about $520) as of December 2012.

Singapore

At a glance

Singapore's mandatory DC system, the Central Provident Fund (CPF), was established in1955to provide financial security for employees in their retirement. The system is comprised of individualized accounts fully funded by both employer and employees. Contributions are distributed among threetypes of individual accounts.

- **Total system assets:** 230,158 million Singaporean dollars (SGD) (*about $181,227 million)* as of 2012
- **Percentage of workers with DC accounts:** over 80 percentof the resident workforce

Types of plans
Until age 55, CPF savings are maintained in three accounts:

- **Ordinary account** saving scan be used for housing, investment, and other approved purposes.
- **Special account** maintains savings that are set aside for retirement and can be used for investment in retirement-related financial products.
- **Medisave account** savings help CPF members meet their own or their immediate family's hospitalization expenses.

The **retirement account** is created for CPF members when they reach the age of 55. Savings from the ordinary and special accounts up to the minimum sum amount (148,000 SGD as of 2013) are transferred to this account.

This amount is set aside for the purpose of providing members with steady income post-retirement.

Source: GAO analysis of foreign agency documents and interviews with Australian officials and industry experts; State Department (base map); Art Explosion (flags).

Note: GAO did not conduct an independent legal analysis of the laws, regulations, or policies of the countries selected for this review.

Highlights of the Spend-Down Phase

DC Spend-Down Options

- **Lump sums:** At age 55, participants may withdraw their CPF savings in excess of the minimum sum of $148,000 SGD (about $116,535) in their retirement account and a minimum of 40,500 SGD (about $31,900) in their medisave account. Participants who do not have savings in excess of the minimums are allowed to withdraw $5,000 SGD (approximately $3,900).

- **Programmed withdrawals:** Prior to 2013, the primary spend-down option was a programmed withdrawal administered by the CPF Board designed to last for approximately 20 years from the participants "drawdown age," which is currently 65.
- **Annuities:** In 2009, Singapore introduced a new government-managed life annuity system, known as CPF Lifelong Income Scheme For the Elderly (CPF LIFE), to address the challenges of increasing life expectancy and an aging population. From 2013, participants with retirement account balances of at least 40,000 SGD (about $31,500) are automatically placed on CPF LIFE. The government offers two types of annuities, a basic and standard plan. The standard plan is the default plan for participants.

  The standard plan provides higher monthly payments as compared to the basic plan, but leaves a smaller bequest for the participant's family and other beneficiaries

Providers

The CPF Board administers the CPF Fund and CPF LIFE. Private insurance companies offer a variety of annuity products in the retail market.

Regulators

CPF Board was established by law to be the trustee and administrator of CPF.

The CPF Board is also responsible for investing participants' savings in special securities issued by the government. The CPF Board works closely with the Ministry of Manpower and other relevant Ministries on policies that affect CPF, even though the power to initiate changes to provisions on CPF schemes rests with the Minister of Manpower.

National Pension System

CPF is the main source of retirement income for workers. Singapore does not have a multi-pillar retirement system that is similar to the United States. There is no state pay-as-you-go social security.

However, there is other government social spending, which indirectly helps retirees with costs, such as health care and housing.

Switzerland

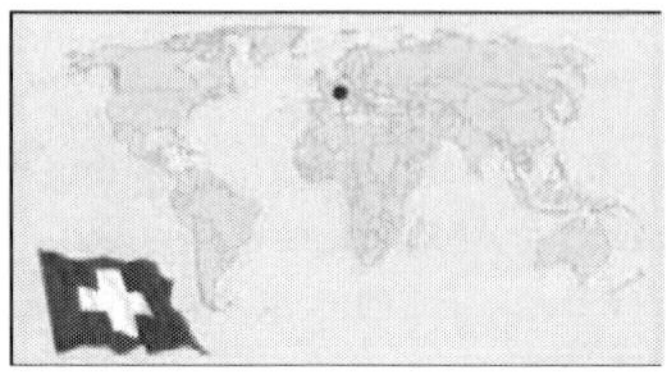

At a glance

Since 1985, Switzerland has had a mandatory system of occupational pension plans for workers with incomes above a certain threshold.[78] Participants do not have a choice of plan, but are placed in their employer's plan. The government regulates minimum contributions, and minimum returns on contributions during accumulation. In 2005, Switzerland extended to some extent coverage of the mandatory system to low-income and part-time workers.

- **Total system assets:** SFr. 625.9 billion dollars (*about $658.8 billion)* as of 2011
- **Percentage of workers with DC accounts:** About 74percent of the labor force

Types of plans

Mandatory occupational plans are administered by independent foundations and may be sponsored by a single employerorgroup of employers. Plans are managed by boards of trustees with equal employerand employee representations. The organization of plans also varies by degree of risk coverage with respect to longevity, premature death or disability.

Autonomous plans bear all the risk.

Autonomous plans with reinsurance hand over some of the risk to a reinsurance company.

Semiautonomous plans include two cases: (1) a plan hands over only the risk of death or disability to an insurance company and consequently still bears the risk of longevity; and (2) the plan buys the old-age pensions from the insurer too.

Fully insured plans are plans in which all the risks are covered by an insurance company.

Savings associations by construction bear no actuarial risks, because only old-age savings are accumulated.

Source: GAO analysis of foreign agency documents and interviews with Australian officials and industry experts; State Department (base map); Art Explosion (flags).
Note: GAO did not conduct an independent legal analysis of the laws, regulations, or policies of the countries selected for this review.

Highlights of the Spend-Down Phase

DC Spend-Down Options

- **Lump sums:** Since 2005, plans have been required to offer participants at least 25 percent of their mandatory retirement savings as a lump sum payment.
- **Programmed withdrawals:** Programmed withdrawals are not available to plan participants.
- **Annuities:** Switzerland requires that annuities have disability and survivor benefits. Pension funds may voluntarily index annuity payments for inflation if they are financially able to do so. In the mandatory portion of the DC system, annuities must be the default option. Although official data are not available, researchers estimate that participants annuitize about 80 percent of their account balance.

Providers

Spend-down options may be administered by independent foundations that manage plans.

Regulators

- **Oberaufsichtskommission** (OAK Commission) came into being in 2012 to harmonize regional oversight and regulation of trust-based pension plans. The Commission also oversees the Guarantee Fund that protects participants in the event that a pension plan becomes insolvent, as well as the Substitute Occupational Benefit Institution that extends coverage to employers who do not meet their pension obligation and those who are not otherwise covered and who wish to voluntarily be covered, such as the self-employed, among others.
- **The Swiss Financial Market Supervisory Authority** is responsible for overseeing insurance companies. It ensures that insurance

companies comply with laws and regulations and fulfill their licensing requirements.

- **The Federal Social Office of Insurance** plans, manages, and monitors Switzerland's social insurance systems to ensure they function effectively.

National Pension System

Switzerland's old age and survivors' insurance (AHV/AVS) is a pay-as-you-go public pension that is funded by payroll contributions and general revenues. The system has two components: an earnings-related public pension funded mainly by payroll contributions and an income-tested supplementary benefit funded by general revenues. Payment amounts for the earnings-related benefit are based on lifetime earnings. Payments in retirement are indexed to prices and earnings. The government coordinates benefits between AHV/AVS and occupational pension plans so that combined, they replace about 60 percent of preretirement income for workers with lower incomes.

United Kingdom

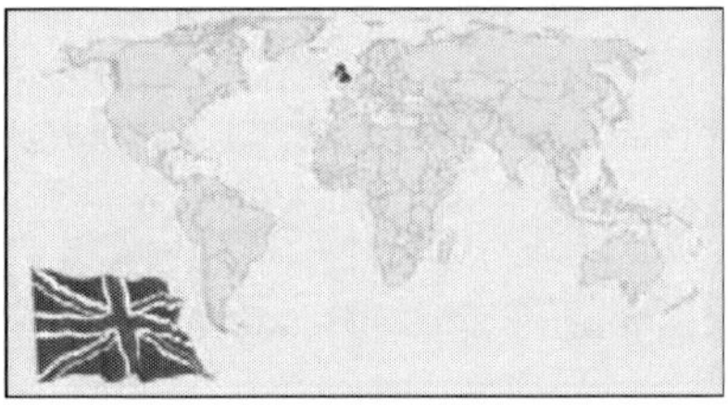

At a glance

Voluntary DC plans make up most of the private pension system in the U.K. An individual may be a member of a number of different pension plans simultaneously. From October 2012, in a staged process, employers were required to automatically enroll their eligible employees into a pension plan—including a new low-cost DC pension saving plan called the National Employment Savings Trust—and provide a minimum contribution.

- **Total system assets:** £385.9 billion (*about $584.70 billion)*as of 2010

- **Percentage of workers with DC accounts**: about 17 percent of employees as of 2012

Types of plans

Trust-based plans (41 percent of DC participants) These are employer-sponsored plans and are usually non-profit entities managed by a board of trustees that typically hire one or more service providers for recordkeeping and investment management services. The trustees are responsible for selecting and vetting the investment options.

Contract-based plans (59 percent of DC participants) For contract-based plans, an employee deals directly with a for-profit service provider that performs both recordkeeping and investment management services. The service provider selects which investment options are available to the participant. These plans are owned entirely by the worker

Source: GAO analysis of foreign agency documents and interviews with Australian officials and industry experts; State Department (base map); Art Explosion (flags).

Note: GAO did not conduct an independent legal analysis of the laws, regulations, or policies of the countries selected for this review.

Highlights of the Spend-Down Phase

DC Spend-Down Options

- **Lump sums:** Participants may take up to 25 percent of plan assets as a tax-free lump sum, subject overall to 25 percent of the individual's lifetime tax-free pension allowance and individual plan rules.
- **Programmed withdrawals:** Under a capped drawdown, participants have the ability to withdraw up to 120 percent of the value of an amount equal to what they would get from a level payment single-life annuity each year. Plan administrators are responsible for reviewing these withdrawals every 3 years and resetting maximum withdrawal limits as needed. Participants who can demonstrate secure income of at least £20,000 (about $30,300) per year may take withdrawals without limit while leaving the balance of the fund invested. This option is known as flexible drawdown.

- **Annuities:** Participants can choose from a number of different options for single-life and joint-life annuities, including level or escalating payments, a guarantee period, and impaired or enhanced rates.

Providers

Plan administrators, which may be a trustee or for-profit provider, are responsible for administering programmed withdrawals. Private insurance companies offer a variety of annuity products in the retail market.

Regulators

- **The Pensions Regulator** is solely responsible for regulating trust-based plans and coordinates with other entities on regulating contract-based plans. It has the authority to oversee the administration of these plans and contributions made to them. For DC plans, its statutory objectives include protecting the benefits of plan participants and promoting and improving understanding of good administration of plans.
- **The Financial Conduct Authority** and **the Prudential Regulatory Authority** share oversight of contract-based plans and financial service providers. The Financial Conduct Authority was the successor to the former authority, the Financial Services Authority. It is responsible for ensuring fairness in the conduct of firms towards their employers and participants, overseeing smaller insurers, as well as asset managers and advisory firms. The Prudential Regulatory Authority, the smaller of the two new entities, is a subsidiary of the Bank of England and tasked with monitoring the safety and soundness of larger insurers, banks, and asset managers.

National Pension System

The basic state pension is a regular payment from the government once an individual reaches a certain age.[79] The amount depends on the number of qualifying years, at least 30 years, individuals have of National Insurance contributions. As of August 2013, the maximum full basic state pension is £110.15 per week (*about $167*). There is also an earnings-related element called the state second pension, which give individuals who earn lower wages or cannot work as much as other the change to receive a better state pension. Under current rules, there is a cap on annual earnings of £40,040 (about $60,700).

End Notes

[1] In 2012, the Advisory Council on Employee Welfare and Pension Benefit Plans, also known as the ERISA Advisory Council, reported that the percentage of private employers offering single-employer DB plans has decreased to less than 9 percent. In contrast, the percentage of private employers offering DC plans has increased to more than 88 percent. See ERISA Advisory Council, *Examining Income Replacement During Retirement Years In a Defined Contribution Plan System*, (Washington, D.C.: December 2012). Another study calculated that 68 percent of workers covered by employer retirement plans only had access to DC plans in 2010 based on U.S. Board of Governors of the Federal Reserve System, Survey of Consumer Finances (1983 and 2010). Alicia H. Munnell, Anthony Webb, and Francis M. Vitagliano, *The Economic Implications of the Department of Labor's 2010 Proposals for Broker-dealers*, Center for Retirement Research at Boston College Working Paper 2013-4 (February 2013).

[2] We have reported on numerous issues that have hampered participants' efforts to save for their retirement, such as fees, participant inertia, and limited financial literacy. For more on these issues, see GAO, *401(k) Plans: Labor and IRS Could Improve the Rollover Process for Participants*, GAO-13-30 (Washington, D.C.: Mar. 7, 2013); *401(k) Plans: Increased Educational Outreach and Broader Oversight May Help Reduce Plan Fees,* GAO-12-325 (Washington, D.C.: Apr. 24, 2012), *401(k) Plans: Improved Regulation Could Better Protect Participants from Conflicts of Interest*, GAO-11-119 (Washington, D.C.: Jan. 28, 2011); and *Retirement Savings: Automatic Enrollment Shows Promise for Some Workers, but Proposals to Broaden Retirement Savings for Other Workers Could Face Challenges*, GAO-10-31 (Washington, D.C.: Oct. 23, 2009).

[3] In addition, in the United States, although DB plan participants must be offered a life annuity option at retirement, there is a growing trend in traditional DB plans to offer participants lump sum payout options. While we note that the challenge of managing the spend-down phase is not solely an issue for DC plans, the spend-down phase in the context of DB plans is outside the scope of this report.

[4] According to the Organisation for Economic Co-operation and Development (OECD), between 1960 and 2010, the average life expectancy at age 65 increased by around 3.9 years for men (from about 12.7 to 16.6 years) and 5.4 years for women (from about 14.7 to 20.1 years), among OECD countries. Furthermore, the United Nations projects life expectancy at age 65 will increase to 20.3 years for men and 24.6 years for women in 2050.

[5] Most occupational retirement plans in Switzerland are hybrid plans that incorporate some DC features, such as individual accounts, within a DB plan structure. Switzerland mandates the rate of return credited to participants' contributions during the accumulation phase as well as the terms for pricing annuities that participants can purchase with these savings.

[6] GAO, *Defined Contribution Plans: Approaches in Other Countries Offer Beneficial Strategies in Several Areas*, GAO-12-328 (Washington, D.C.: Mar. 22, 2012); *Private Pensions: Changes Needed to Better Protect Multiemployer Pension Benefits*, GAO-11-79 (Washington, D.C.: Oct. 18, 2010); and *Private Pensions: Alternative Approaches Could Address Retirement Risks Faced by Workers but Pose Trade-offs*, GAO-09-642 (Washington, D.C.: July 24, 2009).

[7] U.S. Department of Labor, Employee Benefits Security Administration, Private Pension Plan Bulletin: Abstract of 2011 Form 5500 Annual Reports, Version 1.0 (Washington, D.C.: June 2013).

[8] Additionally, ERISA provides for the establishment of the ERISA Advisory Council to advise the Secretary of Labor and make recommendations on the Secretary's functions under ERISA.

[9] Selection of Annuity Providers—Safe Harbor for Individual Account Plans, 73 Fed. Reg. 58,447 (Oct. 7, 2008)(codified at 29 C.F.R. § 2550.404a-4).

[10] Request for Information Regarding Lifetime Income Options for Participants and Beneficiaries in Retirement Plans, 75 Fed. Reg. 5253 (Feb. 2, 2010).

[11] Longevity Annuity Contracts, 77 Fed. Reg. 5443 (Feb. 3, 2012)(to be codified at 26 C.F.R. pt. 1).

[12] NAIC services include providing detailed insurance data to help regulators understand insurance sales and practices; maintaining a range of databases useful to regulators; and coordinating regulatory efforts by providing guidance, model laws and regulations, and information-sharing tools.

[13] Countries we reviewed, including the United States, have taken steps to address the challenges of the accumulation phase for their participants. For example, in order to increase the adequacy of workers' accumulations, Australia is increasing the level of mandatory employer contributions to DC plans, known as superannuation funds, from 9.25 percent in 2013 to 12 percent by 2020. To increase participation and savings in DC and other employer-sponsored retirement plans, in October 2012 the United Kingdom began implementing a mandate on employers to automatically enroll workers into retirement plans and make contributions on their behalf. In the United States, to increase participation in 401(k) plans, Congress, IRS, and DOL took steps to promote the adoption of automatic enrollment and appropriate default investment options for the accumulation phase.

[14] Participants in 401(k) plans may make withdraws on their retirement savings account before retirement under certain limited conditions, typically referred to as leakage. For additional information on the incidence, amount, and relative significance of different forms of 401(k) plan leakages, see GAO, *401(k) Plans: Policy Changes Could Reduce the Long-term Effects of Leakage on Workers' Retirement Savings*, GAO-09-715 (Washington, D.C.: Aug. 28, 2009).

[15] In the United States, programmed withdrawals may be referred to as "systematic withdrawals".

[16] This report provides examples of some annuities in the United States and countries we reviewed, and is not an exhaustive list of all types of annuities.

[17] Variable annuities may include riders, such as guaranteed lifetime withdrawal benefits, to provide various protections or additional features, subject to certain restrictions. In the United States, these newer products have raised some questions about their cost, complexity, vesting rules, and protections of state guaranty associations, among other issues. For additional information about the consumer benefits and risks of newer annuity products in the United States, see GAO, *Retirement Security: Annuities with Guaranteed Lifetime Withdrawals Have Both Benefits and Risks, but Regulation Varies across States,* GAO-13-75 (Washington, D.C.: Dec. 10, 2012).

[18] Longevity risk is the risk of living longer than anticipated at the time of retirement. In such cases, even large savings may be exhausted and prove inadequate.

[19] In addition to government benefits and personal savings, in the United States, other potential sources of retirement income include other financial assets, such as pension income from DB and DC plans and nonfinancial assets such as home equity.

[20] Possible explanations for low savings rates—even in countries where participation in retirement plans is mandatory—include low incomes, which constrain an individual's ability to save for retirement in light of more short-term competing demands, and discontinuous or interrupted work histories, where unemployment or exiting the labor market may be due to childbearing or care giving needs and can interrupt retirement plan contributions. Where participation is voluntary, plan coverage may be low, because employers may not be offering a pension plan, or even if they do, employees may not join, or may choose to opt out if they are automatically enrolled.

[21] Each country's retirement system reflects that country's unique historical and political experience, making generalizations difficult. For example, widespread choice by participants of lump sum payments in Australia may in part reflect the country's long-standing tradition of providing retirement benefits in a single payment, a practice that predates Australia's current mandated DC system.

[22] GAO did not conduct an independent legal analysis of the laws, regulations, or policies of the countries selected for this study.

[23] Chile instituted pathways to all three main spend-down options at the inception of their DC system in 1981.

[24] Retirement plans in Canada are generally regulated at the provincial level, so policies such as locking-in provisions requiring participants to purchase an annuity vary by province.

[25] In the United States, participants who do not have access to annuities or programmed withdrawals through their plan may roll over their account balance into an IRA, where they can develop their own systematic withdrawal strategy, or purchase an annuity in the retail market.

[26] U.S. participants that remain invested in their 401(k) plan past age 70 ½ are required to comply with certain provisions of the Internal Revenue Code that set required minimum distributions from tax-deferred accounts, such as 401(k) plans, generally by April 1 in the year following the year in which the participant reaches age 70 ½. Although considered a minimum distribution, this is different than the formalized programmed withdrawals that other countries offer to participants when retiring prior to age 70.

[27] According to an IRS survey of 1,200 randomly selected plan sponsors, for plan years 2006 through 2008 only 38 percent of 401(k) plans in the United States offered programmed withdrawals, only 19 percent offered qualified joint and survivor annuities, and only 11 percent offered single life annuities. The total percent of plans offering some kind of annuity may be less than 30 percent because the percentages may include plans that reported offering both qualified joint and survivor annuities and single life annuities. Department of the Treasury, IRS Tax Exempt and Government Entities Division, *Section 401(k) Compliance Check Questionnaire*: *Final Report*, (Washington, D.C.: March 2013).

[28] Singapore appointed a committee in 2007 to study the needs of participants and design government-managed annuities. The committee examined mortality data in Singapore and found that more than half of participants were at risk of outliving their programmed withdrawals if they retired at age 65. The committee created retirement simulations comparing retirement provided by the existing programmed withdrawal option against that of the proposed annuities under varying conditions.

[29] The government also cited participants' negative perceptions of annuities as a reason for this change. The government attributed these perceptions in part to a decline in the size of payments from annuities in response to falling interest rates and increases in longevity. The government also attributed negative perceptions to a lack of understanding about how annuities work. Regulators, policymakers, and the pension industry in the United Kingdom have taken steps to raise awareness among participants about strategies for getting more income from annuities, for example, by shopping for annuities that provide larger payments to individuals with certain health conditions or lifestyles that may reduce their longevity. Sales of enhanced annuities, which are annuities that provide larger payments because the annuitant has a shorter life expectancy, have grown rapidly since their introduction in 1995. According to Towers Watson, sales of enhanced annuities increased from £419.6 million ($635.8 million) in 2001 to nearly £4.5 billion ($6.8 billion) in 2012.

[30] In order to take programmed withdrawals without restriction, known as flexible drawdown, participants must document that they have a secure pension—for example, from an annuity—of at least £20,000 (about $30,300) per year. Participants that do not meet this requirement may take capped drawdowns, generally limited to 120 percent of the value of an equivalent single-life level annuity.

[31] According to the financial service provider, in 2011, programmed withdrawals accounted for about £2 billion ($3 billion) in DC plan distributions, whereas annuities account for about £12 billion ($18.1 billion). See Mark J. Warshawsky, *DC Plan Payout Practices and Policies In Canada, Switzerland, U.K., Australia, and Singapore, Towers Watson Insider* (Arlington, VA: January 2013).

[32] See 75 Fed. Reg. 5253 (Feb. 2, 2010). The agencies asked for information on issues such as advantages and disadvantages of receiving benefits in the form of lifetime payments, types of lifetime income products currently available to participants through their plan, and regulatory barriers to offering lifetime income, among other issues. In September 2010, DOL and Treasury held a joint hearing to discuss their request for information and further consider specific issues relating to spend-down options intended to produce retirement income for participants.

[33] For example, one respondent said that IRS rules requiring minimum distributions from 401(k) plans beginning at age 70 ½ can act as a barrier to some lifetime income options such as "deeply" deferred annuities that begin payments at an advanced age, such as 80 or 85. Respondents also described challenges for participants in comparing annuity prices and features. Respondents also cited participants' reluctance to choose lifetime income options even when they are made available, which some attributed to a lack of understanding of these options.

[34] These lifetime payment projections would be based on both the current value of their account and the projected value of their account balance at the normal retirement age. As part of this advance notice of proposed rulemaking, DOL requested comments from the public on whether and how this could be done. Pension Benefit Statements, 78 Fed. Reg. 26,727 (May 8, 2013).

[35] Longevity Annuity Contracts, 77 Fed. Reg. 5443 (Feb. 3, 2012)(to be codified at 26 C.F.R. pt. 1). At present, 401(k) participants who use a portion of their account balance to purchase a deeply deferred annuity may risk violating IRS rules requiring minimum distributions from IRAs beginning at age 70 ½. In April 2013, the Australian government announced that it would encourage the take-up of deferred annuities by providing these products with the same concessional tax treatment that superannuation assets in programmed withdrawal products receive. This reform, which was to apply starting on July 1, 2014, has not yet been implemented.

[36] GAO did not conduct an independent legal analysis of the laws, regulations, or policies of the countries selected for this study.

[37] Australian Securities and Investments Commission, "*Financial Decisions at Retirement: How to make the most of your money and avoid costly mistakes*," accessed July 26, 2013, www.MoneySmart.gov.au.

[38] In particular, the pack highlights the various annuity options, including the enhanced annuities that potentially offer a much higher income for individuals with health or lifestyle conditions that may result in a shorter life expectancy.

[39] ABI is a trade association made up of insurance companies in the United Kingdom. It has over 300 member companies, accounting for 90 percent of the U.K. insurance market. The associations speaks on behalf of U.K. insurers and works work with government, regulators and policymakers—both in the United Kingdom and internationally—to ensure the insurance industry meets the highest standards. ABI, *Consumers in the Retirement Income Market: Code of Conduct on Retirement Choices* (London, U.K.: March 2012).

[40] Kevin Crouch, Ian Sparham, and Richard Fincham, *Pre-retirement Wake-up Pack: Results of Customer Research,* ABI Research Paper No 18 (London, U.K.: ABI, 2009).

[41] Kevin Crouch, Gemma Allen, Fiona Whitehead, Anthony Carter and Rachel Levy, *Retirement Choices: Baseline to Measure Effectiveness of the code of Conduct*, ABI, (London, U.K., May 2013).

[42] Similarly, the Australian Securities and Insurance Commission issued new guidelines in 2011 for DC plans that choose to include retirement estimates in participants' annual benefit statements. These estimates supply the projected retirement savings in a lump sum format at age 65 and the annual stream of income that this lump sum balance is expected to provide from age 65 to 90.

[43] For younger workers, their statements will include estimates of expected pension income under two scenarios where the participant (1) makes no additional contributions and (2) continues contributing until the normal retirement age.

[44] Eduardo Fajnzylber and Gonzalo Reyes, *Knowledge, Information and retirement saving decisions: Evidence from a large scale intervention in Chile*, Working Papers from Adolfo Ibáñez University, School of Government (May 2011).

[45] SCOMP is the Spanish acronym for Electronic Consultation and Offer System for Annuities and Phased Withdrawals.

[46] Although all quotes appear in one document, many participants seem to have difficulty making a decision about the spend-down option by themselves and often use a financial intermediary to help, according to focus groups conducted by the Chilean government. As a result, the government is taking steps to simplify and shorten the document. SCOMP was introduced to increase transparency but also competition among annuity providers.

[47] The Money Advice Service was set up as an independent body in April 2010 as the Consumer Financial Education Body, which was established under the Financial Services Act in 2010 with statutory functions to enhance people's understanding and knowledge of financial matters, and their ability to manage their own financial affairs. The Money Advice Service was launched in April 2011 with online, telephone, and United Kingdom-wide face-to-face services.

[48] Since 2012, most U.K. employers were required to automatically enroll some or all of their workers into a qualifying plan that meets certain minimum standards and pay contributions on their behalf. The U.K. government established the National Employment Savings Trust (NEST) to help employers meet this new requirement. According to a report by the U.K. Department for Work and Pensions, NEST is a low-cost, trust-based, occupational pension scheme focused on people with low to moderate earnings and employers that the existing pensions industry does not serve well.

[49] The administrator of an individual account plan shall provide a pension benefit statement at least quarterly to a participant or beneficiary in a participant-directed 401(k) plan and annually to participants or beneficiaries who have accounts in which they do not have the right to direct the investments of assets in those accounts. 29 U.S.C § 1025(a)(1)(A)(i) and (ii).

[50] Jack Clift, Lauren A. Fleishman-Mayer, Angela Hung, Caroline Tassot, and Joanne Yoong, *Designing Better Pension Benefit Statements: Current Status, Best Practices and Insights from the Field of Judgment and Decisionmaking* (RAND Corporation, April 19, 2013).

[51] Pension Benefit Statements, 78 Fed. Reg. 26,727 (May 8, 2013). As of August 2013, DOL was reviewing comments submitted in response to this advance notice of proposed rulemaking.

[52] Singapore has made annuity payments from CPF LIFE the default option for participants with account balances above a threshold, following recent pension reforms, recognizing that the previous standard practice of programmed withdrawals over 20 years was no longer adequate to ensure lifelong retirement income in light of increasing longevity. Participants with account balances below the threshold, on the other hand, are defaulted into the programmed withdrawal option.

[53] The researchers analyzed the spend-down selections of participants from 10 Swiss companies in the public and private sector between 1996 and 2006. Nine of the 10 companies offered an annuity as the default spend-down option, while the tenth company offered a partial lump sum payment as the standard option. Overall the default option was preferred by more than two-thirds of the sample. Participants at the company that offered a partial lump sum as the standard option, however, only chose an annuity about 10 percent of the time. See Monika Butler and Federica Teppa. "The Choice Between an Annuity and a Lump Sum: Results from Swiss Pension Funds," *Journal of Public Economics*, 91 (2007): 1944-66.

[54] Although people have had the right to shop around for annuities, referred to as "Open Market Option," since 1978, and pension providers have been recommended to include a letter

reiterating that right in the wake up pack since 2004 most people were still using their current pension provider to supply their annuity at retirement.

[55] Around the same time, reforms eliminated taxes on all retirement spend-down options taken on or after age 60. The introduction of key legislation was a significant factor leading to the expansion of the market for programmed withdrawals, according to researchers Bateman, Hazel and John Piggott. "Too Much Risk to Insure: the Australian (non-) Market for Life Annuities," in Olivia Mitchell, John Piggott and Noriyuki Takayama (eds.), *Revisiting Retirement Payouts* (Oxford University Press, 2011), 81-105. In more recent years, sales of annuities in Australia appear to have recovered somewhat. In June 2013, Challenger Limited, Australia's largest provider of annuities projected sales of lifetime annuities for the year of over $220 million (AUD 240 million), approaching the roughly $260 million (AUD 280 million) in annuities sold by all insurers in Australia in 2004, prior to the reforms.

[56] Australian Prudential Regulation Authority, Annual Superannuation Bulletin June 2012 (Sydney, Australia: Jan. 9, 2013).

[57] GAO did not conduct an independent legal analysis of the laws, regulations, or policies of the countries selected for this study.

[58] According to Chilean pensions regulators, both eligibility conditions should be met jointly so if the equivalent amount of 70 percent of income is lower than the maximum pension with a supplement, known as the Pension Solidarity Complement, the participant will not be allowed to take a partial lump sum. For additional information about Chile's pension system, see appendix II.

[59] The rules for accessing a partial lump sum distribution were initially designed as part of early retirement rules. Subsequently, the Chilean government became concerned that the earlier workers retired, the more likely it was that over time it would have to supplement a retiree's benefit with government pension benefits. As a result, the accumulation conditions were revised in 2004 and 2008 from 50 percent of the minimum to 150 percent. In accordance with the introduction of the new solidarity pillar in the 2008 reform, the requirement of financing a pension equal or higher than 150 percent of the minimum pension guarantee was amended to financing a pension equal or higher than 100 percent of the maximum pension with the Pension Solidarity Complement.

[60] When 401(k) plan participants separate from their employers, leaving their plan savings in the plan, rolling or moving the money into a new qualified employer plan, or rolling the money into an IRA, would preserve the tax-deferred status of their plan savings. Lump sum distributions are subject to ordinary income tax. Participants who take an early distribution, those taken before age 59 ½, generally pay a 10 percent additional income tax and incomes taxes on the lump sum distribution amount, in order to discourage the use of plan funds for the purposes other than retirement and ensure that the favorable tax treatment for plan funds is limited to those that are, in fact, used to provide retirement income. See GAO-13-30 for more information.

[61] In Chile, retirees who chose the programmed withdrawal option and exhaust their funds by outliving their actuarial life expectancy could also be eligible for government-guaranteed benefits.

[62] Participants that remain invested in their 401(k) plan past age 70 ½ are required to comply with certain provisions of the Internal Revenue Code that set required minimum distributions from tax-deferred accounts, such as 401(k) plans, generally by April 1 in the year following the year in which the participant reaches age 70 ½.

[63] Selection of Annuity Providers—Safe Harbor for Individual Account Plans, 73 Fed. Reg. 58,447 (Oct. 7, 2008) (codified at 29 C.F.R. § 2550.404a-4).

[64] Selection of Annuity Providers for Individual Account Plans, 72 Fed. Reg. 52,021, 52,023 (Sept. 12, 2007)(to be codified at 29 C.F.R. § 2550.404a-4).

[65] In the United States, annuities offered in pension plans must be offered on a gender-neutral basis. *Arizona Governing Committee v. Norris,* 463 U.S. 1073 (1983). By contrast, annuities offered in the retail market, including IRAs that are not employer-sponsored, are not subject

to the same rule, and these annuities may vary based on gender. Women may find more favorable single-life annuity rates through pension plans, but men may find more favorable rates through the retail market.

[66] See ERISA Advisory Council (December 2012).

[67] It should be noted that, with the exception of Canada, the other countries we reviewed have national regulatory frameworks for insurance. In the United States, insurance regulations are governed at the state level.

[68] We did not assess the adequacy of solvency requirements in the countries we reviewed because this was beyond the scope of this study. Our recent work found that the effects of the financial crisis on insurers and policyholders were generally limited, with a few exceptions. For more information, see GAO, *Insurance Markets: Impacts of and Regulatory Response to the 2007-2009 Financial Crisis*, GAO-13-583 (Washington: D.C.: June 27, 2013).

[69] In Switzerland, where plans are legally required to provide a minimum benefit, plan sponsors have some financial responsibility for annuity payments, according to Swiss regulators.

[70] In the United States, annuities offered in pension plans must be offered on a gender-neutral basis. *Arizona Governing Committee v. Norris,* 463 U.S. 1073 (1983). By contrast, annuities offered in the retail market are not subject to the same rule, and these annuities may vary based on gender.

[71] In general, 401(k) contributions and investment earnings on those contributions are not taxed as income until the employee withdraws them from the plan.

[72] According to APRA officials, the term "guarantee" in this context reflects the policy intent that all could be guaranteed to be included in the mandatory arrangements, as opposed to the historical approach which was that superannuation was provided at the discretion of employers. There is no guarantee of investment performance.

[73] Industry and corporate funds are non-profit entities in that dividends are not paid to shareholders of the trustee company. The directors of the trustee company represent the interests of the fund members and the employer-sponsor(s) in equal numbers, although an independent director may also be appointed.

[74] Australia uses male total average weekly earnings as a measure of average wages.

[75] Women born before1949 become eligible at age 64½.

[76] The Canada Pension Plan operates in every province and territory, except Quebec, which has its own similar pension program, the Quebec Pension Plan.

[77] SCOMP is the Spanish acronym for Electronic Consultation and Offer System for Annuities and Phased Withdrawals. It is an electronic quotation system that shows participants different spend-down options in a comparable format.

[78] Officials in Switzerland said the majority of plans in Switzerland are hybrid plans. These hybrid plans are similar to cash balance plans, which in the United States are legally classified as DB plans because participants' benefits are determined by a benefit formula. However, a cash balance plan has certain features, such as notional "individual accounts" that are similar to DC plans.

[79] The date an individual reaches basic state pension age depends on when he or she was born. For men born before December 6, 1953, the current age is 65. For women born after April 5, 1950 but before December 6, 1953, the age is between 60 and 65. The age men and women are eligible for benefits is expected to increase to age 66 by October 2020.

In: 401(k) Plans and Spend-Down Options ISBN: 978-1-63117-580-0
Editor: Erica L. Chapmann

Chapter 2

DEFINED CONTRIBUTION PLANS: APPROACHES IN OTHER COUNTRIES OFFER BENEFICIAL STRATEGIES IN SEVERAL AREAS*

United States Government Accountability Office

WHY GAO DID THIS STUDY

Service providers play important roles in the U.S. defined contribution (DC) retirement system since they provide services, such as administration and fund management, necessary for operating DC plans. Plan sponsors rely on such providers, yet it is unclear how much participants are paying in fees for these services. Other countries with well-established DC systems face similar issues and some use a variety of approaches to oversee DC plans and service providers and actively focus on fees charged to participants.

GAO was asked to examine, for selected countries' DC systems, (1) how are service providers overseen by regulatory agencies; (2) what key strategies are used to improve fee disclosure to participants; and (3) what key strategies are used to reduce fees? GAO selected Australia, Chile, Sweden and the United Kingdom based on, among other factors, the importance of the DC

* This is an edited, reformatted and augmented version of GAO-12-328, a report to Congressional requesters, dated March 2012.

plans to the country's retirement system and the use of strategies to address service providers' fees. GAO reviewed research on DC plans; collected and analyzed available data; and interviewed government officials, pension experts, service providers, and other relevant representatives in the U.S. and selected countries.

What GAO Recommends

GAO is recommending that Labor consider other countries' experiences as it continues to improve its supervision and requirements related to fee disclosures. In commenting on a draft of this report, Labor generally agreed with the findings and noted that it will consider GAO's recommendations carefully.

What GAO Found

In overseeing DC plans and service providers, regulatory agencies in the countries GAO reviewed use risk-based approaches to target practices deemed most likely to harm participants and to develop preventative measures. While the role of service providers varies, DC plans and service providers in the 4 countries GAO reviewed are overseen by multiple agencies—primarily a pensions regulator and a securities regulator. In each of these countries, the pensions regulator is the agency that regularly collects data on service provider fees, as well as other plan features, which are used to inform their oversight activities. In particular, in several of these countries, the pensions regulator uses these data as part of a risk-based approach to identify service provider practices that may harm participants, instead of relying only on a compliance-based approach. For example, in Chile, pensions agency officials evaluate key features of the DC system, such as the service providers' management of the individual accounts and the composition and role of the board of directors of the service provider. In both Chile and Australia, agency officials said using a risk-based approach enables the pensions regulator to take proactive measures to ensure the DC plans are operating in the best interest of participants. These countries have used risk-based approaches to oversee service providers for a number of years, while the U.S. Department of Labor (Labor) has just begun to develop a risk-based approach in its efforts to oversee U.S. DC plans and service providers.

Other countries have used key strategies to improve the disclosures participants receive about the fees they pay for their DC plans, including presenting disclosures in a consistent, summary format, which has increased transparency. In particular, these countries have made disclosures simpler and more uniform to facilitate comparisons, and one has required that providers highlight the long term impact of fees on participants' account balances. In addition, some countries require that participants receive personalized information about the total amount they pay in fees over a given time period. In Chile, participants not only receive personalized fee disclosures, but they also receive a statement that tells them what they would have paid had they chosen the lowest-cost option. Many of these requirements exceed Labor's disclosure requirements for U.S. DC plan participants.

Other countries use several targeted strategies—including consolidating and streamlining administrative services and establishing low-cost default funds—to keep the fees paid by their DC plan participants at reasonable levels. According to officials in the countries GAO reviewed, it was important to use these targeted strategies because many of their DC plan participants remain disengaged from retirement savings issues despite improved disclosures. For example, in Sweden and the United Kingdom, consolidating administrative functions eliminates the need for fund managers to maintain individual accounts. Representatives from service providers in both countries said this structure allows them to significantly lower their fees. In addition, for individuals who do not actively choose where to invest their contributions, some countries have established low-cost default options through a variety of measures, such as creating a nonprofit entity to run the default fund under a low-cost mandate, increasing the use of online services, and eliminating marketing costs. These countries also take other targeted approaches to lower fees, such as direct regulation of fees.

ABBREVIATIONS

AFP	*Administradoras de Fondos de Pensiones*
DB	defined benefit
DC	defined contribution
EBSA	Employee Benefits Security Administration
ERISA	Employee Retirement Income Security Act of 1974

GDP	gross domestic product
IOPS	International Organisation of Pension Supervisors
Labor	U.S. Department of Labor
NEST	National Employment Savings Trust
OECD	Organisation for Economic Co-operation and Development
SEC	Securities and Exchange Commission
U.K.	United Kingdom

March 22, 2012

The Honorable George Miller
Ranking Member
Committee on Education and the Workforce
House of Representatives

The Honorable Robert E. Andrews
Ranking Member
Subcommittee on Health, Employment, Labor, and Pensions
House of Representatives

Service providers—companies that employers hire to provide the services necessary to operate defined contribution (DC) retirement plans, such as investment management, consulting and financial advice, recordkeeping, custodial or trustee based services for plan assets, and basic customer service—play an important role in the U.S. DC system. As employers who offer DC plans rely on these providers, whose fee arrangements are becoming increasingly complex, it is unclear how much participants are paying for their services. Because the amount of a participant's retirement savings in a DC plan depends on their investment rate of return net of fees, higher direct and indirect fees charged by DC plan service providers can significantly decrease the income available to participants in retirement. Furthermore, oversight of these companies has become more complex because their services and activities may fall within the jurisdiction of multiple regulatory agencies. In order to improve employers' abilities to adequately oversee service providers and monitor the fees participants are charged for their services, the U.S. Department of Labor (Labor) issued an interim final rule in 2010 to increase the transparency of direct and indirect fees in DC plans to plan sponsors. The final rule will go into effect in 2012, and its impact remains to be seen.[1]

Other countries with well-established DC systems face similar issues, and some use a variety of approaches to oversee DC plans and service providers and actively focus on fees charged to participants. Congress is interested in understanding what approaches other countries are using to address these issues compared to the approaches used in the United States. In particular, Congress is interested in whether U.S. regulators can benefit from learning about these alternative approaches as well as the challenges those countries encounter in utilizing and overseeing service providers in their DC plans. In light of this, you asked us to answer the following questions:

1. How are service providers in other countries' DC systems overseen by regulatory agencies?
2. What key strategies are used in other countries to improve fee disclosure to participants?
3. What key strategies are used in other countries' DC systems to reduce fees?

To answer these questions, we selected four countries in which to conduct case studies: Australia, Chile, Sweden, and the United Kingdom (U.K.). To select these countries, we initially reviewed scholarly and nonlegal sources describing the DC retirement systems in other countries. Based on our analysis of relevant research and interviews with pension experts, we identified 10 countries that had DC systems with key features designed to address fees. From those 10 countries, we established selection criteria based on the importance of the DC system to the country's retirement system and the use of strategies to address service providers' fees, among other factors. By focusing on countries in which the DC system is an important pillar of the retirement system, we increased our opportunity to identify practices used in countries with well developed capital markets and where risks to participants are comparable to those faced by participants in the United States. For each of the four countries selected, we reviewed research and other available documentation and interviewed officials and industry experts to determine the role that service providers play in these countries' DC systems and how they are overseen, and to identify the strategies designed to address fees. We obtained broad perspectives on the benefits and drawbacks of the identified strategies from government officials, academics, industry experts, service providers, and other relevant representatives in each country. Where possible, we attempted to obtain and analyze available data on the types and amounts of fees paid in DC plans in those countries. We did not conduct any independent legal analysis to verify the information provided by or about those countries laws or regulations. Appendix I provides additional information on our scope and methodology.

We conducted this performance audit from March 2011 through March 2012 in accordance with generally accepted government auditing standards. Those standards require that we plan and perform the audit to obtain sufficient, appropriate evidence to provide a reasonable basis for our findings and conclusions based on our audit objectives. We believe that the evidence obtained provides a reasonable basis for our findings and conclusions based on our audit objectives.

BACKGROUND

Roughly 40 percent of all U.S. workers participate in pension plans offered by their employers.[2] Under Title I of the Employee Retirement Income Security Act of 1974 (ERISA), employers are permitted to offer their employees two broad types of retirement plans, defined benefit (DB) and DC. Over the past three decades, there has been a general shift by employers away from DB plans to DC plans, the most predominant of which is the 401(k) plan. According to estimates by industry researchers, 51 million American workers were active 401(k) plan participants in 2010 and, by year end, 401(k) plan assets amounted to $3.0 trillion.[3] Unlike DB plans, employers that offer 401(k) plans do not promise employees a specific benefit amount at retirement—instead, the employee and/or the employer contribute money to an individual account held in trust for the employee.[4] Participants direct these contributions to mutual funds and other financial market investments; the amount available at retirement is dependent on, among other things, investment returns net of fees. In this way, 401(k) plan participants have more control over their retirement assets than DB plan participants but also bear the responsibility for ensuring they have adequate retirement savings.

Employers who offer these plans are considered plan sponsors and generally have the responsibility to act prudently and in the best interest of the plan's participants as they hire various outside companies to help run the plan and choose investment options to offer in the plan.[5] Most 401(k) plans allow participants to direct the investment of their contributions, but their choices are generally limited to those investment options their plan sponsor chooses to offer. Participants also pay a number of fees, including expenses, commissions, or other charges associated with operating a 401(k) plan.[6] Fees are charged by the various outside companies that the plan sponsor hires to provide a number of services necessary to operate the plan. Services can include investment management (e.g., selecting and managing the securities included in a mutual fund); consulting and providing financial advice (e.g., selecting vendors for investment options or other services); recordkeeping (e.g., tracking individual account contributions); custodial or trustee services for plan assets (e.g., holding the plan assets in a bank); and telephone or web-based customer services for participants. An investment company, bank, advisor, or insurance company may offer any or all of these types of investment products as plan options to a 401(k) plan. As shown in figure 1, service providers can be used to provide a number of services necessary to operate a 401(k) plan.

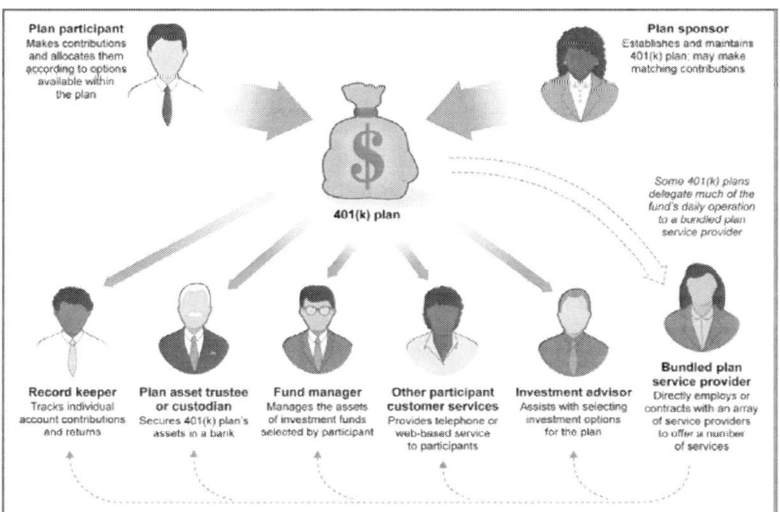

Source: GAO analysis of information from industry practitioners.

Note: Services can be bundled or unbundled with investment management services or advisory services. Under a bundled service arrangement, the plan sponsor hires a company that provides multiple services directly or through subcontracts. Under unbundled arrangements, the sponsor uses a combination of service providers.

Figure 1. Structure of Service Provider Arrangements in 401(k) Plans.

401(k) service providers are typically overseen by various U.S. federal and state regulators. Labor's Employee Benefits Security Administration (EBSA) has numerous responsibilities related to the oversight of 401(k) plans and protection of 401(k) participants' assets,[7] including educating and assisting plan sponsors and participants, investigating alleged violations of ERISA, responding to requests for interpretations of ERISA through advisory opinions and rulings, and making determinations to exempt transactions that would otherwise be prohibited under ERISA. However, as we have previously reported, Labor's civil enforcement efforts for plan service providers are largely limited by the extent to which the provider functions as a fiduciary under ERISA,[8] and many providers are reported to commonly structure their relationships with sponsors in a manner that avoids being subject to these fiduciary standards.[9] To carry out its enforcement duties, Labor has offered voluntary compliance programs and has relied primarily on leads from participants, plan sponsors, and other agencies to conduct targeted investigations on specific types of plans and service providers.[10] In addition to Labor's role, the specific investment products commonly offered in 401(k) plans fall under the authority of the applicable securities, banking, or insurance regulators. These regulators include the Securities and Exchange Commission (SEC), federal and state banking agencies, and state insurance commissioners as follows:

- SEC, among other responsibilities, regulates securities markets and issuers, including mutual funds, under various securities laws.
- Federal agencies charged with oversight of banks—primarily the Federal Reserve Board, the Office of the Comptroller of the Currency, the Federal Deposit Insurance Corporation, and state banking agencies—oversee bank investment products.
- State insurance agencies generally regulate insurance products. Some investment products may also include one or more insurance elements, which are not present in other investment options. Generally, these elements include an annuity feature and interest and expense guarantees.[11]

Labor published final regulations on October 20, 2010, to improve U.S. participant fee disclosure, as summarized in table 1.[12] These regulations require that plan sponsors provide participants core information about investments available under the plan, including performance and fee information, prior to investing and at least on an annual basis thereafter, in a chart or similar format designed to facilitate investment comparisons. Pursuant to these new regulations, participants will receive information about pertinent administrative expenses, individual expenses, and investment-related fees and expenses that they may pay throughout the year. Participants will also receive quarterly statements on plan fees and expenses deducted from their accounts along with a description of the services for which the charge or deduction was made.

In addition to the United States, the U.K., Australia, Chile, and Sweden each have extensive DC pension systems. However, in drawing comparisons between countries, it is important to recognize the significant social and economic differences that exist among them and with the United States. While the economies of the U.K., Australia, Chile and Sweden can be characterized as market-based, the U.K. and Sweden generally have more extensive and generous social welfare provisions than that of the United States.[13] As shown in figure 2, the size of each country's economy is far smaller than that of the United States as measured by gross domestic product (GDP). The standard of living, as measured by GDP per capita, ranges from $15,040 in Chile to $46,860 in the United States.[14] In addition, pension assets as a share of GDP varies from 73 percent in Chile to 239.8 percent in Sweden, and DC assets as a share of total pension assets from 5.6 percent in Sweden to 100 percent in Chile.

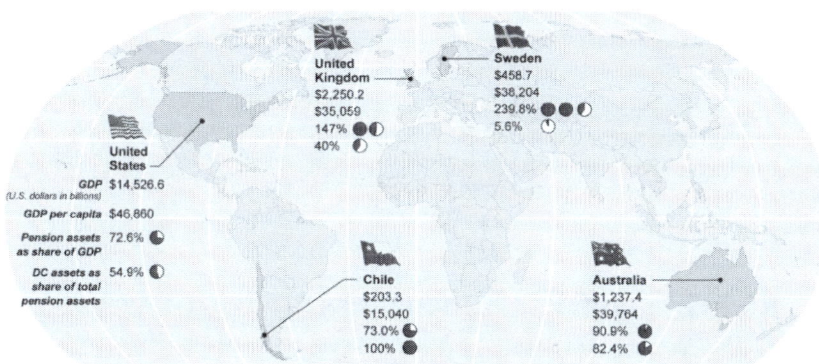

Source: IMF World Economic Outlook Database September 2011, and OECD StatExtracts, Funded Pension Indicators (statistics) extracted on October 23, 2011, government agency officials in foreign countries; Art Explosion (flags); National Atlas (base map)

[a] Total population estimates for these countries in 2011: Australia: 21.8 million, Chile: 16.9 million, United Kingdom: 62.7 million, United States: 313.2 million, Sweden: 9.1 million (see CIA World Factbook).

Figure 2. Economic Data for the United States, Australia, Chile, Sweden, and the United Kingdom, 2010a.

Table 1. Labor's 401(k) Participant Fee Disclosure Requirements

Annual statements	*Administrative fees.* An explanation of the fees and expenses for general plan administrative services and how these fees will affect the balance of a worker's account. These fees may include legal, accounting, trustee, recordkeeping, and other administrative fees and expenses associated with maintaining the plan
	Individual fees and expenses. An explanation of any fees and expenses charged to the balance of a worker's account on an individual basis, rather than on a plan-wide basis. These fees are associated with a service or transaction that an individual may select and may include fees and expenses for plan loans, processing qualified domestic relations orders, investment advice, and brokerage windows[a]
	Investment-related fees. For each investment option in the plan, pertinent performance information, fees and expenses, and investment restrictions: • *Variable investments.* The amount (in percent and per $1,000) of fund management fees and any shareholder fees • *Fixed investments.* The fixed or stated rate of return and any shareholder fees.
	Statement on effect of fees over time.
Quarterly statements	*Administrative fees.* Actual type and amount (in dollars) of plan administrative fees charged
	Individual fees and expenses. Actual type and amount (in dollars) of individual fees and expenses charged

Source: GAO summary of Department of Labor regulations, 75 Fed. Reg. 64,910.

[a] Brokerage windows are self-directed investment options in which participants can invest in individual stocks or mutual funds.

In addition, each country's DC system is slightly different based on their different economic and political conditions. Table 2 has key features of each country's DC system.

Risk-Based Oversight Helps Some Countries' Regulatory Agencies Monitor Service Providers and Could Inform Labor as It Improves Its Oversight Approach

Service Providers' Role and Oversight

As in the U.S. DC system, service providers in the countries we reviewed play an important role and perform a range of administrative and investment management functions. The structure and role of service providers in each country's DC system varies, as described in table 3. For example, in Australia and the U.K., DC plans can be offered through different arrangements and the role of service providers varies accordingly. In some cases, the plan is run by a nonprofit entity managed by a board of trustees with representation from both employers and workers. In other cases, the plan is managed by a for-profit financial service provider with the employer playing little or no role. To address potential conflicts of interest, financial industry representatives in Australia told us that these plans, known as retail plans, have licensed trustees who are legally obliged to act in the best interests of participants, such as by reviewing the use of internal service providers. Agency officials said they look for documentation of this review of the use of service providers.

Table 2. Key Features of Case Study Countries' DC Systems

Dollars in billions USD			
Country	**Description of DC system**	**Types of plan(s)**	**Approximate total DC assets in 2010**
Australia	Australian employers have been required to make a minimum contribution to a pension account based on a percent of employees' salaries, since 1992. The current requirement is 9 percent.	Plans in Australia are generally set up as trusts. There are three types of trust-based private pension plans available in the Australian market: industry-wide or single-employer plans with nonprofit trustees; retail plans with for-profit trustees; and self-managed accounts, where the individual is his/her own trustee.	$853
Chile	Since 1981, Chilean workers have been required to contribute 10 percent of their salary, plus an additional contribution to cover certain fees, to a DC pension plan.	Workers choose among for-profit pension service providers known as AFPs (*Administradoras de Fondos de Pensiones*) for their individual DC pension plans. There are currently 6 AFPs workers can choose from.	$148
Sweden	All Swedish workers and their employers have been required to contribute a total of 2.5 percent of the covered portion of workers' salaries to individual DC accounts in the Premium Pension System, which was introduced in pension reform passed in 1998.[a]	Individual accounts in the Swedish system are all part of one plan managed by a government-run clearinghouse, the Swedish Pensions Agency.	$62

Table 2. (Continued)

Country	Description of DC system	Types of plan(s)	Approximate total DC assets in 2010
United Kingdom	Voluntary DC plans make up most of the private pension system in the U.K. An individual may be a member of a number of different pension plans simultaneously. Since 2001, all employers with five or more workers, who were not already sponsoring a pension plan, have been required to designate a stakeholder pension provider and offer it to their workers.[b] From 2012 to 2017, all employers will be required to automatically enroll eligible employees into a pension plan and provide a minimum contribution. Employers who do not offer a qualifying pension plan will be able to auto-enroll their employees into a new national DC pension option, called the National Employment Savings Trust (NEST).[c]	There are two fundamental types of DC pension plans available in the U.K. private pension system: trust-based schemes, which are set up by employers, and contract-based schemes, which may be facilitated by the employer but are owned entirely by the individual.	$1,320

Source: GAO analysis of foreign documentation and interviews with industry experts

[a] An additional 16 percent of the covered portion of workers' salaries are contributed to notional, or non-financial, DC plans, which are designed to mimic DC plans where the pension depends on contributions and investment returns. However, in these notional accounts, the return that contributions earn is a notional one determined by average earnings growth and adjusted as necessary, not the product of investment returns in the markets. Moreover, notional DC plans are basically pay-as-you-go financed (i.e. current contributions pay for current benefits). However, Sweden also currently has a substantial buffer fund, holding assets equivalent to 25 percent of GDP, which the regulator projects will co-finance benefits beyond 2040.

[b] Stakeholder pensions are a type of low-cost personal pension with limits on the charges that providers can impose.

[c] The pensions regulator noted that a number of new trust-based plans not associated with particular employers have been launched to compete with NEST in the new auto-enrollment market.

Table 3. Key roles of DC Service Providers by Country

	Key roles of DC service providers	Recordkeeping services	Investment management services	Trustee or trustee-like services
Australia	In general, trustees of Australian plans have authority to hire service providers, but the service providers' roles vary based on the type of plan: *Industry-wide and single-employer plans:* nonprofit entities managed by a board of trustees that typically hire separate service providers for recordkeeping and investment management services.	√	√	
	Retail plans: an employee deals directly with a for-profit service provider which performs recordkeeping, investment management, and trustee services.[a]	√	√	√
	Self-managed plans: set-up by employees and entail establishing a trust and a bank account. The trust is required to be audited by a third party. Up to four people can be in the trust. The employees are the trustees and can select their investment options. The employees may hire a financial adviser or other experts to select investment options.	√	√	
Chile	In Chile, service providers play a key role in running the DC plans. For-profit pension service providers known as AFPs (*Administradoras de Fondos de Pensiones*) directly manage participants' individual accounts and provide both recordkeeping and investment management services. Each AFP offers five different investment funds with varying risk levels subject to specific regulations. AFPs hire external fund managers to provide some of these investment options.	√	√	
Sweden	The Swedish Pensions Agency, a government agency, contracts with service providers to perform investment management for the DC portion of the public pension system.[b] Nearly 800 investment options are available for participants to choose from		√	

Table 3. (Continued)

	Key roles of DC service providers	Recordkeeping services	Investment management services	Trustee or trustee-like services
United Kingdom	In the U.K., the key roles of service providers vary based on the type of plan: *Trust-based plans:* nonprofit entities typically hire one or more service providers for recordkeeping and investment management services. The plan trustees are responsible for selecting and vetting the investment options. NEST, a new nationally available plan, operates in this way.	√	√	
	Contract-based plans: an employee deals directly with a for-profit service provider which may perform both recordkeeping and investment management services. The service provider, in conjunction with an advisor or employer if necessary, selects which investment options are available to the participant.	√	√	√

Source: GAO analysis of foreign agency documentation and interviews with industry experts.

[a] According to agency officials, service providers for retail plans are often part of a conglomerate where related companies provide services for the plan.

[b] The DC portion of the public pension system is known as the Premium Pension.

In each of the countries we examined, some of the service providers are large U.S.-based companies. For example, in Australia and the U.K., representatives of U.S. service providers we spoke with said they perform a variety of functions ranging from consulting services to managing the plan, including both administrative and investment management functions. In contrast, because of the structure of the DC systems in Chile and Sweden, U.S. service providers play a more limited role and generally provide fund management or other consulting services.

While the role of service providers varies, in most of the countries we reviewed DC plans and service providers are overseen by multiple agencies—primarily a pensions regulator and a securities regulator, as described below. Moreover, in Australia and the U.K., where DC plans can be offered through different arrangements, the oversight structure differs based on the type of plan.

- In Australia, for industry-wide, single-employer and retail pension plans—called superannuation plans—the pensions regulator licenses trustees and oversees their management of the plan, including the use of service providers. Self-managed superannuation plans, on the other hand, are primarily overseen by the tax authority. In conjunction with both of these agencies, the Australian securities regulator oversees financial services, including the disclosure of fees for superannuation plans.
- In the U.K., the pensions regulator oversees trust-based plans and their use of service providers, while the securities regulator oversees the investment funds offered in these plans—particularly disclosures—and acts as the primary regulator for individual contract-based plans.[15] For other contract-based plans designated by employers but administered by for-profit service providers, oversight is jointly conducted by both the pensions regulator and the securities regulator.
- In Chile, the pensions regulator intensively oversees plan providers, including issuing licenses for them to participate in the system. On an ongoing basis, the pensions regulator monitors plan providers for compliance with investment option guidelines, reserve requirements, fee structure, and other requirements. The Chilean Ministry of Finance and the Central Bank coordinate with the pensions regulator on certain issues related to investment regulation.
- In Sweden, the pensions regulator administers the plan and establishes terms of participation for investment fund providers. The Swedish securities regulator, meanwhile, oversees the funds offered in the Swedish pension system, along with other investment products and services provided by the financial services industry. In addition, the securities regulator monitors the Swedish Pensions Agency as the annuity provider for the DC system.

Risk-Based Oversight Approach

In each of the four countries we reviewed, regulators use a risk-based approach to oversee DC plans and service providers and identify practices that may harm participants.

In general, risk-based oversight involves developing a structured approach to identify potential risks faced by the DC system and assessing the processes in place to address those risks.[16] For example, in Chile, agency officials evaluate key features of the DC system, such as the service providers' management of the individual accounts and the composition and role of the service providers' board of directors and investment committee. Based on this assessment, the regulatory agency decides if supervisory action is necessary and, if so, what type of action—ranging from issuing guidance to imposing sanctions or withdrawing licenses to operate as a DC plan provider—is appropriate.

Based on discussions with these countries' officials and a review of the International Organisation of Pension Supervisors (IOPS) risk-based supervision literature, using a risk-based approach allows regulatory agencies in other countries to identify potential problems before they become widespread and take proactive measures to address them.[17] For example, in both Chile and Australia, agency officials said risk-based supervision enables the pensions regulator to implement supervisory actions proactively to ensure DC plans are operating in the best interests of participants. A review of supervisory approaches by IOPS also notes that a risk-based approach is preventative in nature and increases the likelihood that significant problems will be identified and addressed at an early stage. For example, in the U.K., as part of their risk-based approach agency officials said they conduct an annual survey of plan trustees to help identify potential problems which could include high fees or conflicts of interest.[18]

In addition, in Australia, the pensions regulator's approach is forward-looking in that it actively monitors and assesses the performance and situation of DC plans on an ongoing basis and then estimates the plans' capacities to manage risk.[19] Based on this assessment, the pensions regulator determines what actions need to be taken, such as more frequent and detailed data collection or working with the plan to restructure their operations or merge with another plan.[20]

In addition, agency officials and a review of supervisory approaches by IOPS cite a number of other beneficial effects of using a risk-based approach. For example, using a risk-based approach, regulators can take the following actions:

- *Allocate scarce resources more efficiently to target key risks.* By prioritizing risks, the agency can determine which DC plans or service providers require more attention and spend minimal effort on issues that pose the least threat or likely have little impact. For example, in Australia, the need for the pensions regulator to monitor a relatively large number of institutions may make compliance-based supervision either too costly or ineffective. As a result, the pensions regulator focuses on identifying higher-risk institutions that require more intensive oversight. Likewise, officials from the securities regulator in Sweden said the main advantage of risk-based supervision is the more efficient use of resources. Specifically, these officials told us that the Swedish securities regulator would not be able to conduct in-depth reviews of every fund management service provider every year; instead, the official believed that investigating only those potentially problematic service providers, as indicated by the data the regulator collects, better utilized its limited resources. In addition, the U.K. established a new risk-based pensions regulator in 2005 after a review of the previous regulator revealed inefficiencies with the compliance-based approach. In particular, the review found that numerous low-risk cases typically overwhelmed the high-risk, high-profile cases.

- *Adapt to the changing nature and complexity of financial risks.* By evaluating potential risks on an ongoing basis, a risk-based approach provides regulators flexibility to adapt to the continuing evolution of financial investment options. For example, in Chile, the pensions regulator introduced a risk-based approach to adapt to the increasing complexity of the financial markets.[21] Chile has gradually been relaxing investment regulation and, at the same time, strengthening the governance of plan providers by ensuring sound risk management practices and internal controls. Such practices include requiring plan providers to develop an investment policy and establish committees to monitor and address investments and conflicts of interest. Furthermore, in Australia, in addition to ongoing oversight of DC plans, the pensions regulator conducts ad hoc studies to address new and emerging trends, such as a study prompted by the financial crisis to increase their monitoring of the liquidity of DC investment funds.
- *Encourage pension plans to have sound risk management practices.* By assessing the processes in place for the plan to manage key risks, the regulator provides an incentive for plans to adopt good practices to improve their risk rating. For example, in its supervision of the superannuation industry, the Australian pensions regulator's main priority during 2010 and 2011 was to encourage more robust governance and risk management practices. To do so, it has been

strengthening the capacity of some of its analysts and utilizing industry-wide analysis techniques to advise plans about the particular aspects of risk management for which they may lag behind their peers, which the regulator has found to be helpful in focusing the plans on areas where improvement is needed.

- *Promote trust and confidence in the regulator's role*. Establishing a systematic and consistent approach enhances confidence in the regulator's methods and in the pension system in general. For example, the Australian pensions regulator's use of a structured framework for risk assessment in pension plans in its risk-based approach is reported to have improved the consistency of its oversight outcomes by allowing for more standardized reactions to supervisory issues across a large number of service providers and supervisors, which enhances the pension industry's confidence in the regulator's methods and procedures.

Table 4 below summarizes the main differences between risk-based and compliance-based approaches.

Table 4. Main Features of Alternate Regulatory Approaches

Risk-based	Compliance-based
Regulators • identify potential risks, • assess mitigating factors and proper management of all risks, and • target scarce supervisory resources at supervised entities deemed as most at risk	Regulators • focus on breach of laws, rules, and regulations, and • give the same degree of attention to all funds
Approach is preventative, forward-looking, flexible	Approach focuses on a given point in time, often relies on complaints
Supervised pension plans or service providers have an incentive to strengthen risk management	Supervised pension plans or service providers focus on compliance with rules rather than risk management
Regulators can benchmark supervised entities and assess overall industry	It is difficult for regulators to get meaningful comparisons across supervised entities

Source: GAO summary of International Organisation of Pension Supervisors documentation.

Moving from Risk-Based to Compliance-Based Supervision

International Organisation of Pension Supervisors (IOPS) guidance to pensions supervisors in its Toolkit for Risk-Based Pensions Supervision, includes a discussion about the interaction and complementary nature of risk-based and compliance-based supervision. According to IOPS, [m]oving towards RBS [risk-based supervision] is often accompanied by the deregulation of strict rules and a move towards a more 'prudential' approach to regulation, applying more high level principles. Yet RBS can be applied whether a rules-based or a principles-based form of regulation is in place. There is no one, perfectly deregulated model which all countries should be striving towards. Some pension systems (e.g. mandatory systems) requiring greater levels of protection are likely to apply more comprehensive rules than others. Whether risk is controlled via rules or via prudential regulations simply changes the nature and focus of the supervisory approach. Likewise, there is no need for an either/or choice between RBS and a more traditional or rules-based supervisory approach (i.e. simply checking for compliance with regulations). RBS does not mean having no rules or compliance procedures in place… Both methods can and should be blended according to the nature of the pension system which is being overseen. The key is to find the mix which is most appropriate according to the nature of the pension system, the capacity of the supervisory authority, and the level of development of the pension industry

Source: IOPS Toolkit for Risk-based Pensions Supervision, Module 0.

IOPS notes that the introduction of risk-based supervision should be viewed as a movement along a continuum from one extreme of complete reliance on a compliance-based system to one where the emphasis of supervision is a function of risk, as described in the text box below. In addition, according to IOPS, regulators in many countries have been or are planning to utilize risk-based supervisory approaches, but implementation varies. For example, the Chilean pensions regulator has maintained some compliance procedures around quantitative investment limits in addition to its assessments of AFPs' (*Administradoras de Fondos de Pensiones*) investment risks. Thus, a risk-based approach may contain compliance-based elements. IOPS also notes that the regulator's active communication with the pension community can help it overcome the challenges associated with moving to risk-based oversight from compliance-based oversight.[22]

In general, risk-based oversight requires extensive data collection and analysis to identify individual risks at the entity level, as well as systemic risks that occur as a result of changes in the financial, economic, or social environment, and affect all or most of the entities in the DC system. However, the implementation of a risk-based approach varies and the regulators in the countries we reviewed adapt it to the unique features of their DC system, as described in the text box below.

Examples of Risk-Based Supervision by other Countries' Pensions Regulators

Australia

The pensions regulator identifies main risk areas and evaluates how plans are addressing them, which include (1) board membership and management of the plan, (2) market and investment risk, and (3) operational risk (recordkeeping and management of outsourcing contracts). For each risk category, the pensions regulator scores plans from low (zero) to high (4). For example, to assess investment risk, it evaluates whether the plan has a clear investment strategy. A plan rated as "extreme risk" would have a high concentration of assets in one product market and high exposure to volatility. For the board of the plan, the regulator's staff evaluates key factors, such as the quality, skills, and experience of all directors, whether the board meets composition and independence requirements, and potential conflicts of interest at the board level. In determining the risk ratings, the regulator's staff collects and analyzes financial data and other information on a regular basis. Superannuation plans with at least $50 million in assets are required to report quarterly performance data, in addition to the standard annual reporting. The pensions regulator uses quarterly data on returns to check for unusual trends, which may prompt further investigation. If necessary, staff also conduct on-site visits with plans and service providers.

Chile

The pensions regulator evaluates key aspects of the DC system, such as management of the plan provider, investment risk, and operational risk. The limited number of plan providers, six as of 2011, allows the regulator to closely monitor the operation and performance of each one, including risk areas specific to a plan provider.

For example, the regulator collects and analyzes data from plan providers on a daily and ad hoc basis on investment holdings and other issues. Pension industry representatives said that the regulator's data collection efforts help to keep the agency knowledgeable about the system and well-positioned to act when necessary.

United Kingdom

The pensions regulator uses a standard model for risk assessment, but does not apply individual risk scores to each plan on an annual basis because of the large number of plans the agency oversees—nearly 46,000 DC plans and over 1,000 hybrid plans with some DC benefits. Instead, the regulator collects information annually from large DC plans and up to every 3 years from smaller DC plans, which inform the regulator's risk-based approach.

Source: GAO analysis of foreign agency documentation and interviews with officials and industry experts.

Note: The Swedish pensions regulator operates the Swedish Premium Pension system and has direct agreements with service providers, from which it collects information on service provider fees and transaction costs, among other things. The Swedish securities regulator takes a risk-based approach in its oversight of Swedish funds that can be included in the Premium Pension system.

Labor's Oversight Approach: Risk-Based versus Compliance-Based

In contrast to the other countries we reviewed, in the United States, Labor has not yet targeted enforcement efforts based on broad, ongoing risk assessments, or assessments of key areas of noncompliance with ERISA. Rather than using a risk-based approach, Labor has primarily relied on reports or complaints obtained from participants, plan sponsors, the media, and other agencies to conduct targeted investigations on specific topics.

As we reported in 2007 and 2011, this approach generally limits Labor to leads identified by these sources and not those potential violations that may be more complex or hidden in nature.[23] To address these limitations, in 2011 Labor officials told us that they have taken preliminary actions to develop a more risk-based approach to enforcement.

For example, agency officials said Labor has adopted the following measures:

- Labor has begun implementing routine compliance examinations. These examinations will allow Labor to assess the effectiveness of its current enforcement efforts and allow better targeting of its limited resources.
- To address risk assessment trends, Labor has established a National Enforcement Library to serve as a "knowledge management" tool for the agency, which will provide information on current trends and emerging developments in plan investment and management.

While Labor is taking preliminary steps to improve its oversight, the more extensive risk-based approaches taken by the countries we reviewed allow them to take preventative measures and address the shortcomings of relying only on complaints.

For example, the Chilean pension regulator started introducing a risk-based approach in 2006 to adapt to the increasing complexity of financial markets given that it is not feasible to monitor all the operations of financial institutions.

Agency officials said that adopting a risk-based approach allows them to take action that is preventative in nature. Furthermore, in the U.K., officials from the pensions regulator said that they rely, in part, on participant complaints and whistle-blowing to identify problems, but this is not effective with DC plans because of the asymmetry in information between service providers and participants.

In general, officials said that participants tend to be disengaged and, even if they review disclosures, many lack the knowledge to understand the information provided to them. As a result, officials said that participants do not understand enough about their plans to identify potential problems.

By adopting a risk-based approach instead, the pensions regulator, in its view, has been able to identify the greatest risks and work with plans to resolve issues.[24]

Fee Disclosure Strategies Improved Transparency in Some Countries, and Similar Strategies Could Benefit U.S. Participants

Fee Disclosure Formats

Some other countries with well-developed DC systems, including Chile, Sweden, and Australia, have taken steps to make fee disclosures simpler and more comparable, requiring that disclosures to participants be presented in consistent, summary formats.

Officials in each of these countries told us that improved fee disclosures provide their participants transparency about the fees they are paying for their DC plans, which may help participants make informed decisions about their investments.[25]

Consistent with the approaches taken by these countries, research based on behavioral economics indicates that useful disclosure approaches include standardizing the types of fees and the formats in which they are presented in order to facilitate comparisons across different investment options.[26] For example, Chile, Sweden, and Australia reported making the following changes to their fee disclosures to increase transparency from previous disclosures:

- To increase awareness of fees among Chilean workers, the Chilean pensions regulator requires that statements sent to participants every 4 months use more understandable vocabulary and provide a summary of fees paid in the participant's statement. The summary includes graphics and a table with a comparison of fees across plans, as well as a personal pension projection (which translates the current account balance into an estimated total benefit amount received at retirement given certain assumptions). Fees included in the participant statements are expressed as a percentage and in Chilean pesos and reflect all administration fees and some fund management fees that a participant may pay.[27]
- In Sweden, the Swedish Pensions Agency sends fee information to all Premium Pension participants as part of an annual, individualized participant statement. This includes the total administration and fund management fee that participants paid and summary information on fund management fees for each fund a participant is invested in that allow comparison among the options chosen.[28] Funds are required to

report their fees to the Swedish Pensions Agency, and the Swedish Pensions Agency consolidates it in a standard format for participants. In addition, the Swedish Pensions Agency publishes fund management fees for all investment options in the system on its website, which further allows individuals the opportunity to compare investment fund fees. A Swedish official noted that transparency is higher now than it was 10 years ago and that awareness of the importance of fees seems to have increased among participants and the media.

- The Australian government has made improvements to its participant disclosures. Participants receive a Product Disclosure Statement when they first join an Australian superannuation plan and periodic statements at least annually thereafter that itemize fund earnings and how much has been taken out of a participant's account in aggregate administrative and investment management fees.[29] As described in table 5, 2005 regulations have enhanced and streamlined the fee disclosures that participants receive and provide greater certainty and consistency by defining the fees and costs that were included in a standardized fees and costs template. Officials noted that these improved disclosures have increased the transparency and comparability of data and felt that participants were more aware of cost issues with respect to their superannuation plans. For example, Australian officials said that the purpose of requiring the "example of annual fees and costs table" in participant disclosures is to create a more easily comparable format for fees across different service providers.

As described in table 5, Australian Product Disclosure Statements are required to include a "consumer advisory warning box" which encourages consumers to shop around and contains an example that displays the effect of fees and expenses on a participant's account.

This example, depicted in figure 3, shows the actual impact of fees over time in Australian dollar amounts, demonstrating to participants why they should pay attention to even small differences in fees.

Table 5. Australia's Fee Disclosure Requirements

Product Disclosure Statements (provided before consumer purchases product)	**Fees and costs template**	A standardized fee template that simplifies the disclosure of fees and costs and allows for more effective comparison across products. This template includes information about the amount of a fee or cost, how the fee or cost is charged, the frequency of the payment, its timing, and whether it is negotiable.
	Additional explanation of fees and costs section	A separate section that includes additional important information about fees and costs, such as adviser compensation, transactional and operational costs, how to negotiate lower fees, and details about any fee changes. This information is kept separate in order to preserve the simplicity of the fees and costs template.
	Example of annual fees and costs table	Provides an illustrative example of fees and charges in a balanced investment option[a] for a typical account balance and level of contributions (e.g., AUD 50,000 account balance and an annual contribution of AUD 5,000).
	Consumer advisory warning box	Emphasizes to consumers the importance of considering the benefit they will receive from the services they will pay for. It also shows the compounding value of fees and costs and how a small difference in a fund's investment performance or fees can have a significant effect on long-term investment returns.
	Shorter Product Disclosure Statement requirements[b]	Maximum 8-page Product Disclosure Statement with prescribed minimum font size and section headings so consumers can easily find important information in the Product Disclosure Statement and compare across products.
Periodic statements (ongoing disclosures provided at least annually)	**Other management costs**	An item that shows the approximate amount, stated in Australian dollars, of management costs that were not paid directly out of a worker's account but may have affected their investments. This may include costs of investing through a trust or other structure that holds underlying investment assets, which ensures that layers of management costs are captured when there is a chain of entities involved.
	Total fees paid by participant	An item that shows a single dollar amount—in Australian dollars—that includes the total fees a member or product holder paid during the period. This amount does not include transactional and operational costs that may have been incurred.

Source: GAO summary of foreign agency documentation.

[a] A balanced investment option is defined as the investment option in the plan with an asset mix of 70 percent higher-risk investments and 30 percent lower-risk investments, or the investment option in the plan that is as close as practicable to this asset mix. This option was considered to be the most appropriate for comparison purposes across plans. If the plan does not offer a balanced investment option, the example table is to be based on the plan's default investment option. If the plan offers neither, the example should be based on the investment option with the most funds invested.

[b] These requirements for superannuation plans are still being implemented. According to the Australian Securities and Investments Commission, all new plans and certain existing plans had to comply as of June 22, 2011, but all other Product Disclosure Statements have to comply by June 22, 2012.

DID YOU KNOW?

Small differences in both investment performance and fees and costs can have a substantial impact on your long term returns.

For example, total annual fees and costs of 2% of your fund balance rather than 1% could reduce your final return by up to 20% over a 30 year period (for example, reduce it from $100 000 to $80 000).

You should consider whether features such as superior investment performance or the provision of better member services justify higher fees and costs.

You may be able to negotiate to pay lower contribution fees and management costs where applicable. Ask the fund or your financial adviser.

TO FIND OUT MORE

If you would like to find out more, or see the impact of the fees based on your own circumstances, the **Australian Securities and Investments Commission (ASIC)** website (www.fido.asic.gov.au) has a *[superannuation or managed investment fee]* calculator to help you check out different fee options.

Source: Mercer Legal Pty Ltd.

Note: Example provided by Mercer Legal Pty Ltd. According to Mercer representatives, the example includes prescribed wording and format required by Australian law (regulations made under the Corporations Act 2001) for superannuation product disclosure as of November 2011. Bolded box added for emphasis.

Figure 3. Consumer Advisory Warning Box in Australian Product Disclosure Statement.

Personalized Fee Information

Some countries require that participants receive personalized information about the total amount they pay in fees over a given time period and a comparison of that personalized information to a benchmark (lowest-cost fee or fee paid by the average participant) for additional context. For example, in Sweden, as shown in figure 4, the participant statement sent annually includes standard information on administrative and fund management fees paid for each fund.[30] The "fund fee percent" is presented for each fund the participant invested in, and an "average pension saver" fund fee percent is provided for comparison. In addition, the total amount subtracted for administrative and fund fees from the participant's account balance for the year is disclosed.

Your pension accounts

Your savings towards the national public pension during 2010.

Changes in 2010 in SEK	Income pension	Premium pension
Value 2009-12-31	823 514	70 761
Pension credit for 2009	50 480	7 887
From deceased contributors	582	54
Administration and fund fees	- 383	- 330
Change in value	-23 885	8 258 *
Value 2010-12-31	850 308	86 630

*539 SEK is included here as interest on pension credit for 2009.

To date you have saved this much towards your national public pension **936 938 SEK**

Your premium pension

In the table you can see the development of your premium pension during 2010 and the fees that you pay for fund management. You can compare this with the information for the average pension saver. New premium pension credits are invested according to the breakdown of your latest choice.

Premium Pension Account 2010-12-31	Value SEK	Change in value per cent	Fund fee per cent	*Chosen allocation per cent	Current allocation per cent
Equity Fund Sverige	29 895	18	0,19	30	35
Equity Fund Global	22 286	14	0,35	25	26
Interest Fund Sverige	7 087	2	0,14	10	8
Generation Fund	20 812	11	0,19	25	24
Medical Products Fund	6 550	1	0,50	10	7
Total	86 630	13	0,26	100	100
The average pension saver		*12*	*0,32*		

Keep in mind that high fees can entail a less change in value for you as a saver

Source: Swedish Pensions Agency

Note: These excerpts from an example of an annual Swedish participant statement simply and clearly show the total amount—in Swedish kronor—that the participant paid in fees. In addition, the disclosure document also shows the participant's fee detail for the specific funds in which a participant has chosen to invest their Premium Pension contributions, by fund and in total, and provides the total fund fee as a percent for the average pension saver for comparison purposes. Bolded boxes added for emphasis.

Figure 4. Example of Sweden's Fee Disclosure Requirements for Premium Pension Participants.

Personalized fee disclosure example

(Individual with a taxable income of US $760 as of November 2011)

FEE COSTS

If someone would make monthly contributions for 12 months, the total fees paid to the system would be:

A.F.P.	Total annual percentage fee		Annual difference with respect to the least costly AFP
	%	(US$)	(US$)
CAPITAL	1,44	131	27
CUPRUM	1,48	135	31
HABITAT	1,36	124	20
MODELO	1,14	104	—
PLANVITAL	2,36	215	111
PROVIDA	1,54	140	36

Source: Superintendence of Pensions, Chile.

Note: Every four months, Chilean participants receive a pension disclosure that includes a table of personalized costs, such as the one seen in this excerpt, which shows—in Chilean pesos and as a percent—the total fees they would pay in any of the plans in which they could invest their pension contributions and the annual difference between the plans' fees. For the purpose of this example, the Chilean pensions supervisor has provided the table in U.S. dollars based on the exchange rates in November 2011. Bolded box added for emphasis.

Figure 5. Example of Chile's Fee Disclosure Requirements.

In Chile, participants not only receive personalized fee disclosures, but they also receive information about what the participant would have been charged if they belonged to the other five plans, including the lowest-cost option as shown in figure 5. Thus, the participant can see the specific difference in fees they are paying through their plan compared to the lowest-cost option.[31]

Labor's Fee Disclosure Requirements

In their current form, Labor's fee disclosure improvements will not actually show U.S. participants the effect of fees on their accounts over time. Instead, Labor's recently issued regulations will require that participant disclosures include generic language on the long-term impact of fees and expenses, including that the cumulative effect of fees and expenses can reduce the growth of a participant's account, as shown in figure 6. This generic language does not include the actual effect of fees over time in dollar amounts.

In addition, the fee disclosures U.S. participants will receive under Labor's new fee disclosure requirements do not provide participants the total amount that they have actually paid in one place, or a cumulative cost amount. Labor's new participant disclosure regulations will require that participants receive quarterly statements on some plan fees and expenses deducted from their accounts along with a description of the services for which the charge or deduction was made. However, fund management fees are not included in this quarterly requirement. For these fund management fees, as shown in figure 7, participants will receive annual disclosures that report them as a percentage and as a dollar amount (based on a $1,000 account balance), but do not specifically report the dollar amount of fees paid by a participant based on their account balance. In order to discern their total fee, participants will have to calculate the fund management fees they paid based on their account balance and the information provided in the annual disclosure, and add the fees separately disclosed in their quarterly statements to that calculated amount.

> The cumulative effect of fees and expenses can substantially reduce the growth of your retirement savings. Visit the Department of Labor's Web site for an example showing the long-term effect of fees and expenses at http://www.dol.gov/ebsa/publications/401k employee.html. Fees and expenses are only one of many factors to consider when you decide to invest in an option. You may also want to think about whether an investment in a particular option, along with your other investments, will help you achieve your financial goals.

Source: U.S. Department of Labor.

Note: Labor's recently issued regulations will require that participant disclosures include generic language on the long-term impact of fees and expenses, an example of which is shown in this excerpt. This example states that the cumulative effect of fees and expenses can substantially reduce the growth of a participant's account but does not show, in dollar amounts, how a participant's account balance could differ given differing fee levels. The link to Labor's website, which is provided in this example, does show, in dollar amounts, how a participant's account balance could differ given differing fee levels, but participants do not specifically see this level of detail in their fee disclosures.

Figure 6. Example of Labor's 401(k) Participant Disclosure Requirement Demonstrating the Effect of Fees.

Table 3—Fees and Expenses			
Name / Type of Option	Total Annual Operating Expenses As a %	Total Annual Operating Expenses Per $1000	Shareholder-Type Fees
Equity Funds			
A Index Fund/ S&P 500	0.18%	$1.80	$20 annual service charge subtracted from investments held in this option if valued at less than $10,000.
B Fund/ Large Cap	2.45%	$24.50	2.25% deferred sales charge subtracted from amounts withdrawn within 12 months of purchase.
C Fund/ International Stock	0.79%	$7.90	5.75% sales charge subtracted from amounts invested.
D Fund/ Mid Cap ETF	0.20%	$2.00	4.25% sales charge subtracted from amounts withdrawn.

Source: U.S. Department of Labor.

Note: Bolded box added for emphasis.

Figure 7. Example of Annual Fee Disclosure Requirements for 401(k) Participants under Labor's New Regulations.

While Labor has made recent improvements to U.S. participants' fee disclosures, fee disclosure improvements made by some of the countries we reviewed may provide more transparent disclosures. U.S. participants typically do not receive the simple, useful, and more targeted information about their DC retirement plans and investment options that is provided to participants in Chile, Sweden, and Australia, which could be why recent research shows that U.S. participants have misconceptions about the fees they pay.[32] For example the Australian consumer advisory warning box shows how a small difference in a fund's investment performance or fees can have a significant effect on long-term investment returns. (See figure 3.) In addition, participants in Sweden and Chile received personalized fee information that shows the exact amount, in Swedish kronor and Chilean pesos, that participants paid, without any need for calculation on the part of the participant. (See figures 4 and 5.)

TARGETED STRATEGIES USED BY SOME COUNTRIES LOWER FEES

Consolidating and Streamlining Service Providers' Administrative Functions

Officials in the countries we reviewed told us they have been successful at reducing administrative and fund management fees by consolidating and streamlining administrative functions, such as account processing, recordkeeping, and participant communications.[33] Moreover, each country uses a slightly different approach to provide this efficiency. For example, Sweden and the U.K. have each consolidated administrative services into one entity, which has improved administrative efficiency by eliminating duplicative processing functions and allowed that entity to complete bulk trades with fund providers.[34] Representatives from service providers in both countries said this structure allows them to significantly reduce their costs—and thus to lower their fees—because they only receive one aggregate transfer each day from the administrator, they do not have to maintain individual accounts, and they do not have to market to participants. As shown in figure 8, Sweden's centralized entity is a government body and it requires that providers rebate a substantial portion of their charges to participants in order to acknowledge the cost savings at the fund level of not completing those consolidated administrative activities.[35] Because of this consolidated structure, average total administration and fund management fees that the participant pays are about 0.50 percent,[36] which have been shown to be lower than the rest of the Swedish market and low by global standards.[37]

The Importance of Using Direct Measures to Address Fees

While simpler, personalized disclosures increase transparency and can help participants make informed decisions about their accounts, officials and industry experts in the countries we reviewed noted that disclosure alone has not been successful at reducing fees. In particular, officials and industry experts in each country said that many participants are disengaged and do not make active decisions, even when it would lower their fees. Thus, officials in these countries told us that they have decided not only to improve participant disclosures but also to take complementary approaches to reduce fees, since fees can significantly reduce participants' account balances over time. Officials in some of the countries we reviewed emphasized the importance of taking direct measures to lower fees—research shows that a failure to ensure adequate retirement savings may increase reliance on public retirement programs, which would further increase governments' future financial burdens.

Source: GAO analysis of foreign agency documentation and interviews with officials and industry experts.

Figure 8. (Continued).

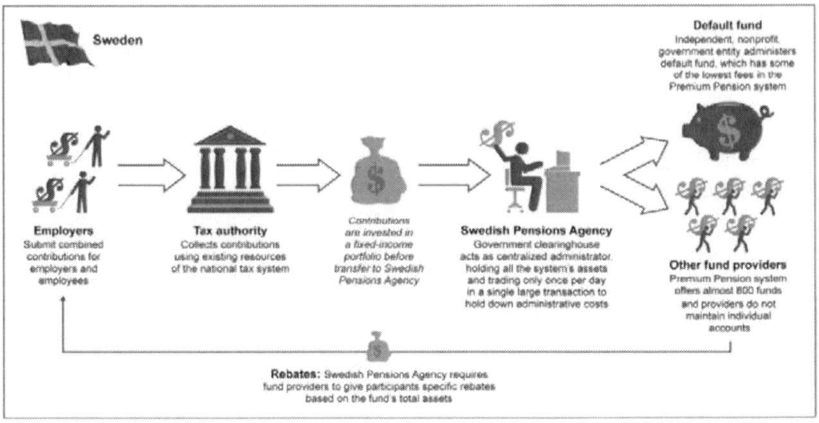

Source: GAO analysis of foreign agency documentation and interviews with industry experts.

Figure 8. The Structure of Sweden's Premium Pension System Helps Lower Administrative and Fund Management Fees.

As described in figure 9, the U.K. has also set up its nationally available, low-cost plan by consolidating administrative functions, but it has used one for-profit service provider for administration and a limited number of additional for-profit service providers for fund management.[38] U.K. plan representatives said that consolidating administrative functions has increased their scale and bargaining power, which has allowed them to attain lower fees from service providers. In addition, the U.K. plan will be highly automated and provide for many self-service functions, which they expect will lower costs. This low-cost plan is expected to particularly help low-income workers employed by small employers, and experts we spoke to noted that they anticipate huge cost savings for those workers if their employers offer the plan. Total administrative and fund management fees for this nationally available DC plan will be 0.30 percent, which is generally lower than fees participants pay for other DC plans offered in the U.K.—which typically range from 0.40 to 2.00 percent.[39]

In contrast to Sweden and the U.K.'s approach to consolidate administrative functions into one entity, the Australian pensions regulator has encouraged mergers among superannuation plans that have lowered administration fees for some participants and has also recently proposed standardized requirements to streamline administrative services within each service provider that are intended to lower fees for all participants.

Table 6. Australia's Proposed Regulations to Reduce Costs through a Variety of Methods

Reform	Proposed measures
SuperStream reforms	• Implement new data and e-commerce standards for superannuation transactions to improve the quality of data in the system • Allow the use of tax file numbers as the primary locator of member accounts • Encourage the use of technology to improve processing efficiency, removing substantial manual processing • Improve the way plan-to-plan rollovers are processed and the way contributions are made by developing standardized forms and supporting electronic transactions • Help participants avoid paying unnecessary fees on multiple accounts by streamlining the process to consolidate accounts, such as through automatically consolidating any accounts with less than AUD 1,000 to the current active account unless the member opts out and allowing superannuation plans to search the Australian Taxation Office registers for any lost or unclaimed superannuation and advise the member that they may wish to consolidate their superannuation accounts • Enhance new employee enrollment process where employees will be able to access a listing of all their superannuation accounts from Australian Taxation Office online to assist with exercising choice • Establish an advisory governance body to advise on the implementation and maintenance of the standards
Securing Super reforms	• Provide better information about the amount and timing of superannuation payments to employees
	• Provide notification from plans to members on whether contributions have or have not been received

Source: GAO summary of Australian government publication.

For example, Australia will adopt data standards to make superannuation transactions more timely and efficient, will reduce the number of accounts per member, and will make other changes, as shown in table 6. Industry experts thought that modernizing and standardizing administration, including enhanced use of technology, would effectively decrease fees in the Australian superannuation system, and a consultant estimated the new requirements would decrease fees by about 7 percent. Furthermore, industry officials estimated that the proposed requirements would save the Australian superannuation system up to AUD 1 billion annually.[40]

Default Options Are Designed to Charge Low Fees

For participants who do not actively choose where to invest their contributions, some countries have established default options that lower fees in a variety of ways, such as creating a public option default fund, increasing the use of online services, and eliminating marketing costs. For example, the Swedish government established an independent, nonprofit entity to administer the default investment fund. Officials noted that fund management fees for this fund are low compared to the other funds in the system—the equity portion charges a 0.15 percent fee and the bond portion charges a 0.09 percent fee—because it is a public option mandated by the government to be cost-effective and because it has sufficient size to command low fees from outsourced service providers.[41] A default fund official also noted that this low fee is made possible through a government subsidy for the default fund's startup costs, implemented to lessen the inequities in fees charged across generations. According to this official, 2011 is the second year in a row that the default fund generated a surplus; by 2016, the fund expects to repay the government loan and, as a result, to further decrease fees.

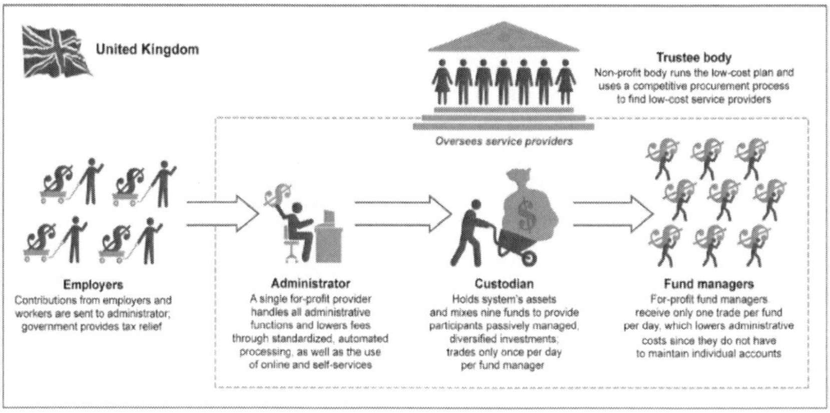

Source: GAO analysis of foreign agency documentation and interviews with industry experts.

Figure 9. The United Kingdom Has Structured Its Nationally Available Plan to Reduce Administrative and Fund Management Fees.

Table 7. Australia's Proposed MySuper Default Products Will Be Limited to Certain Fees

Type of fee[a]	Description	Amount allowed
Administration fee	These are fees for recordkeeping and general services required for day-to-day administration of the plan. They are typically disclosed as a fixed dollar amount, in Australian dollars.	No limitation
Investment fee (including a performance-based fee)	These fees are typically expressed as a percentage of assets and represent the cost of managing the plan's assets, including custody and indirect expenses.	Performance-based fees are subject to the following limitations:[b] • A reduced base fee that reflects the potential gains the investment manager receives from performance-based fees, taking into account any fee cap; • measurement of performance on an after-tax and after-cost basis; • an appropriate benchmark and hurdle for the asset class reflecting the risks of the actual investments; • an appropriate testing period; and • provisions for the adjustment of the performance-based fee to recoup any prior or subsequent under-performance (for example, high water marks, clawbacks, vesting arrangements, and rolling testing periods).[c]
Buy and sell spreads	Implicit when a fund buys or sells assets, the buy and sell spread is the difference between an asset's entry price and exit price and is a cost incurred by the fund each time it invests or withdraws funds.	Limited to provider's cost recovery

Table 7. (Continued)

Type of fee[a]	Description	Amount allowed
Exit fee	Fees charged when an individual removes his/her investments from the plan (at retirement or to move into another plan).	Limited to provider's cost recovery
Switching fee	Fees charged when the participant changes his/her investment options within the plan.	Limited to provider's cost recovery

Source: GAO analysis and summary of Australian government publication.

[a] MySuper default products are limited to these fees; MySuper providers are prohibited from charging any other fees, including hidden fees such as trailing commissions—fees paid to advisors each year the participant owns the fund so that the advisor will review the participant's holdings and provide advice. Plan trustees can charge for certain member-specific costs, such as account splitting following a family law decision.

[b] If a performance-based fee arrangement does not contain each of these provisions, the MySuper trustee must be able to justify that the differing arrangement continues to be in the best financial interests of the members of the MySuper product.

[c] High water marks provide that payment of performance fees is conditional on exceeding the maximum fund value for which the fund manager has already received performance fees. Clawbacks require recent performance fees to be paid back to plan participants if the fund suffers subsequent significant losses. Vesting arrangements lock performance fees, wholly or partially, for a period of time to align the fund manager's interests with the plan participants' interests. Rolling testing periods require that performance fees should be calculated on an ongoing basis so a longer period can be used to assess performance.

Similarly, in Chile, all new entrants are defaulted to the lowest-cost plan provider for 2 years as determined by a bidding process. Most participants do not monitor or actively manage their accounts and officials noted that they tend not to switch service providers to get lower fees. The total cost for the plan provider that won the first bidding process is considerably lower than for some other providers—1.14 percent of salary[42] compared to a range of 1.36 to 2.36 percent of salary for other providers.[43] Even though costs for each plan provider differ, service providers stated that plan investment returns were very similar. Furthermore, Chilean officials reported that new participants who have no or low accumulated balances actually achieve a higher return in the low-cost plan provider than if they had chosen the provider with the best yield, which showed that these participants could save on fees without sacrificing returns. However, while the bidding process has lowered fees for new participants, it has not done so for existing participants because most have stayed with their current provider even though these providers did not lower their fees. Officials said they expect future bidding processes to lead to more competition and, thus, lower fees even further for future participants or participants who decide to switch providers.

In Australia, government officials and industry experts said recently proposed requirements for a new, simple, cost-effective default superannuation product, called MySuper, should result in considerably lower fees.[44] An industry consultant estimated that the MySuper proposals could charge around 0.66 percent of assets, which is about 30 percent less than the current industry average. In addition, MySuper default funds will have a single, diversified investment strategy and a standard set of fees. As seen in table 7, officials expect to see reduced fees since certain types of fees will be limited, but they have not explicitly capped fees.[45] All fees must be included under the standard descriptions, which officials said will allow workers, employers, and market analysts to compare funds more easily. Employers will have better information to assist with selecting a default fund and confidence that any MySuper product will meet minimum standards and offer a cost-effective superannuation plan for their workers.[46] It will also ensure that workers do not pay for any additional features or services they do not need or use. In particular, the MySuper product is restricted from including investment advice as a standard service, which an industry expert said is not widely used by participants.

Other Targeted Approaches

The countries we reviewed have also taken other targeted approaches which have been effective at lowering fees, such as the following:

- *Direct regulation of types or amounts of fees.* Chile and Australia have reduced some fees participants pay by directly banning certain fees or types of fees, while the U.K. has seen certain fees decline because of explicit fee caps. Chile officials told us that they banned fees as a percent of assets and fixed fees because some participants' account balances were severely diminished after periods of little or no contributions.[47] Similarly, Australia has recently moved to restrict commission-based compensation for investment advisors because they noticed that some participants were being charged ongoing fees by advisors to plans but were not receiving ongoing advice. In the U.K., on the other hand, officials recognized that total fees could be lower for participants and implemented certain plans with explicit fee caps. According to officials we spoke to, although not many participants actually utilized these plans, their presence increased competition in the industry and substantially lowered fees.[48]

- *Direct regulation of certain service provider practices.* Australia and Sweden have moved to ban practices that have increased fees. Australia has proposed a ban on “flipping”—when a service provider rolls a participant’s superannuation plan account into a personal plan, for which fees can be 2 to 3 times higher. Government officials focused on this practice because it is typically done without participants’ consent. Sweden also recently banned the practice of investment advisors changing funds for their customers en-masse via computerized systems, which some advisors were doing frequently without providing individualized advice to their customers. According to Swedish representatives, this practice significantly increased transaction costs and inflated fees for some participants.
- *Increased education and licensing requirements for certain occupations.* In Australia and Chile, increased requirements for education and licensing of different industry stakeholders have decreased fees. In Australia, officials told us that increased requirements for plan trustees led to significant consolidation among certain types of plans.[49] For example, an official told us that nearly 4,000 of those plans collapsed to 400 or 500 through mergers. According to an industry expert, many of these consolidations occurred because trustees of certain superannuation plans may have decided that they had less expertise in running a superannuation plan than running their business. According to agency officials, the increased size of plans after consolidation may have led to decreased fees. In Chile, on the other hand, increased requirements for pension advisors have reduced the number of advisors and have imposed stricter rules for switching accounts among AFPs. Prior to the increased requirements, Chilean officials told us that advisors often used abusive practices to provide incentives for workers to switch accounts, such as giving workers part of the advisor’s commission or other bribes and filling out the worker’s form with potentially

fraudulent signatures, which also caused large system costs. One service provider noted that the education and licensing requirements prohibited these practices and, thus, reduced overall costs in the system and fees for participants over time. The stricter rules for switching accounts also led to mergers and acquisitions among AFPs with less market share, which increased the size of the remaining AFPs, allowing them to charge lower fees and still remain competitive.

- *Other strategies.* The countries we reviewed have also taken other targeted approaches that have reduced fees, which are summarized in table 8, but the reduction in fees from any one of these approaches may not have been significant for all participants in the DC systems.

Table 8. Other Strategies That Have Reduced Fees

Country	Strategy	Description
Chile	Participants can only invest through one plan (AFP)	The Chilean system avoids duplicative administrative costs associated with multiple accounts.
United Kingdom	Pensions Quality Mark	Introduced by the National Association of Pension Funds, an industry group of plan professionals and service providers, this voluntary mark sets a standard of excellence for employer-offered DC plans that employers can use to promote their plan. One component of the mark limits fee levels.
	Efforts to improve participant selection of annuity provider	The national Money Advice Service, which was started by the U.K. securities regulator but has since become an independent organization, publishes annuity prices on its website. It also provides information to help participants select the type of annuity best suited for them since the data shows that 2 in 3 participants select their DC plan provider for an annuity even though the cost can be up to 40 percent higher than with other providers.

Source: GAO analysis of foreign agency documentation and interviews with industry experts.

Conclusion

The countries we reviewed have taken a variety of steps to oversee service providers and improve fee disclosures. However, these nations typically did not rely primarily on improved transparency to lower fees paid by participants, but combined transparency improvements with other targeted approaches to reduce fees. Despite important social, economic, and institutional differences between the United States and these countries, the key strategies these countries used to effectively lower fees offer some potential options for the U.S. experience. Given that a number of major U.S. service providers operate in several of the countries we reviewed and have adjusted to the regulatory requirements of these strategies, similar practices could be feasible in the United States. In addition, given the size of the U.S. DC system, implementation of some of the innovative approaches to reduce fees taken by these other countries may prove to be less expensive and more efficient for U.S. service providers. As more American workers rely on DC plans for their retirement savings and since excessive fees can have an adverse effect on net savings, it is important that Labor continue to address the impact of fees on participants. Consideration of approaches used by these countries that have proven to be successful could help Labor in this effort.

Labor could learn from the positive experiences of other countries as it improves its supervisory approach and refines its participant disclosure regulations. In particular, regulatory agencies in the countries we reviewed have developed and already put into practice risk-based supervisory practices that could help Labor as it moves toward a risk-based approach in its own enforcement efforts. Given the significant role of service providers in the U.S. DC system and the complexity of fees charged for their services—including the impact of fees on participants' account balances—it is important that Labor effectively oversees plans' use of service providers. Similarly, Labor's current efforts to improve participant disclosures are a promising development, but may be strengthened by taking steps to evaluate their effectiveness, costs, and potential effect on coverage, and, as necessary, making further improvements. In this respect, the efforts taken by several countries that have improved their disclosures by making them more personalized and significantly highlighting the long-term impact of fees could prove instructive, relevant, and positive to the U.S. experience. If no action is taken to monitor and respond to potential shortcomings in participant disclosures, some participants will continue to be unaware of the fees they are paying and the long-term impact of those fees on their retirement savings.

RECOMMENDATIONS FOR EXECUTIVE ACTION

We recommend that the Secretary of Labor take the following two actions:

- Consider other countries' experiences as Labor continues its efforts to develop a risk-based approach in supervising DC plans and their service providers, such as adopting risk-based oversight practices developed by the International Organisation of Pension Supervisors and used by the countries we reviewed that have helped them better oversee their DC plans.
- Consider recent international initiatives to improve fee transparency to assess their relevance and utility for U.S. 401(k) plan participants, such as improvements that provide summarized and personalized fee information and that show the effects of fees over time.

AGENCY COMMENTS AND OUR EVALUATION

We provided a draft of this report to the Departments of Labor, State, and the Treasury, and the Securities and Exchange Commission (SEC) for their review and comment. SEC and the Department of State did not provide comments. The Departments of the Treasury and Labor provided technical comments, which we have incorporated where appropriate. The Department of Labor (Labor) also provided written comments. Overall, Labor generally agreed with our findings and noted that it will consider our recommendations carefully as it derives insights from its own multinational pension research and policy discussions.

Regarding our recommendation on risk-based supervision, Labor agreed that other countries' experiences can sometimes be useful in evaluating U.S. policies and programs but highlighted some differences that exist among the private pension systems of the United States, Australia, Chile, Sweden, and the U.K. In general, we agree that the voluntary and heavily employer-based U.S. system has its own unique institutional and operational features—as does each other system we reviewed—and the diversity of each system makes it impossible to apply risk-based supervisory principles in a strict, uniform manner. This is why we explain that risk-based supervision can be, and has been, implemented to varying degrees along a continuum with compliance-based supervision. Specifically, Labor pointed out that the U.S. DC system is voluntary and, unlike its foreign counterparts, U.S. regulators must take account of the risk that employers will simply decline to sponsor retirement plans. We note that other countries have implemented risk-based supervision within voluntary systems and that, even in some of the more compulsory systems we reviewed, the fund provider or trustee involvement may not be required. For example, the Australian pensions regulator's risk-based approach has not driven away trustees of over 4,000 regulated superannuation plans even though it is not mandatory for those trustees to offer plans—it is only mandatory for employers to remit a portion of their employees' salaries to those plans.

Labor also noted that U.S. plans are not licensed and that Labor's foreign counterparts generally have more discretion to intervene and require actions as part of supervision of their licensed entities, whereas Labor generally must establish a violation before it can compel action. While we understand the distinction Labor makes between a regulator's authority over licensed entities versus that over nonlicensed entities, we note that Labor does have the authority to influence U.S. fiduciaries by providing guidance, publishing regulations, targeting enforcement efforts, and, if necessary, seeking legislative changes. Risk-based supervision is focused on how the regulator can better utilize its limited resources to oversee regulated entities regardless of the type of retirement savings vehicle they offer—it does not increase employers' risks. In fact, irrespective of the supervisory approach taken, regulators must decide the level of compliance complexity that the regulated entities must meet. Consequently, we believe that Labor could encourage employers to sponsor plans while balancing the complexity of compliance to avoid excessive burden. Overall, we commend Labor on starting to pursue a risk-based approach that is suitable to U.S. circumstances as part of its overall enforcement strategy—in concert with the other enforcement efforts Labor detailed in its letter.

Regarding our recommendation on fee disclosure, Labor agreed that it will look into the global experiences described in our report for possible areas of improvement as it monitors the implementation of its new regulations. Labor commended us on the excellent summary of fee transparency activities being implemented in the countries we reviewed, and noted that it is open to learning from global experiences that help drive down costs and improve retirement saving results for workers. Although Labor was impressed that regulators in the countries we reviewed tended to focus on the same issues that Labor did in its recent efforts to improve fee disclosure, it did not believe it was an appropriate time to propose changes to recent fee disclosure regulations. We continue to believe that it is important to look at what has worked well in other countries as Labor moves forward in evaluating the implementation of its new regulations. Regarding our fee disclosure findings, Labor was unclear whether the countries we reviewed had as complex of a fee structure—particularly with respect to indirect fees—as is common in the United States, whether the reported amounts for actual fees paid were precise or estimates, or what such disclosures cost. We note that there are indeed indirect fees charged in these countries, and that they are already trying to find ways to disclose to their plan participants actual fees paid in as precise a way as possible within their cost structures because they believe that their plan participants benefit from such disclosures. We continue to believe that Labor should consider our findings as a starting point for considering whether to require the disclosure of total actual fees paid within its own parameters, including cost to participants. Finally, Labor noted that its disclosure regulations require a statement about the effect of fees over time and a reference to Labor's website where examples can be found. As we state in our report, participants continue to be unaware of the fees they are being charged, which is why we believe it is more useful for the example to be given directly after such a statement, as other nations, like Australia, currently do.

Charles A. Jeszeck
Director
Education, Workforce, and Income Security Issues

APPENDIX I. OBJECTIVES, SCOPE, AND METHODOLOGY

We were asked to answer the following questions: (1) How are service providers in other countries' defined contribution (DC) systems overseen by regulatory agencies? (2) What key strategies are used in other countries to improve fee disclosure to participants? (3) What key strategies are used in other countries' DC systems to reduce fees?

To answer these questions, we selected four countries in which to conduct case studies: Australia, Chile, Sweden, and the United Kingdom (U.K.). To determine which countries should be used as case studies, we conducted an initial broad review of DC systems in a larger sample of countries. In conducting this initial review, we analyzed relevant nonlegal research and interviewed pension experts to identify 10 countries that had DC systems with key features designed to address fees. Specifically, we obtained comparative and country-specific studies of DC systems published by academics; the Organisation for Economic Co-operation and Development (OECD), whose review also included non-OECD countries; and other industry experts, such as the International Organisation of Pension Supervisors. We solicited recommendations from representatives of the OECD, government officials, academics, industry practitioners, and representatives of industry groups. We then examined the characteristics of each country's DC system for key elements designed to address service providers' costs. From the 10 countries, we used the following selection criteria to select 4 countries for in-depth case studies:

- DC retirement plans are an important pillar of the country's retirement system. By focusing on countries in which the DC system is an important pillar of the retirement system, we increased our opportunity to identify practices used in countries with well developed capital markets and where risks to participants are comparable to those faced by participants in the United States.
- DC retirement plan regulators use explicit strategies to address and oversee service providers' costs. The selected countries as a group should address all of the key strategies we have identified, although no single country needs to address all of them.
- The country was identified through our research and the consensus of external experts as having strong potential for yielding useful lessons for the U.S. experience.
- The country's DC retirement plan is not duplicative. Where similar plans exist in multiple countries, we will select the one that best addresses the other selection criteria.

For each of the four countries selected, we determined how service providers are overseen by regulatory agencies and identified the key strategies designed to improve fee disclosure to participants and reduce fees by reviewing nonlegal research and other available documentation and interviewing officials and industry experts. Specifically, we interviewed industry groups, service providers, and government officials from each country, as well as academics, representatives from the OECD and The World Bank, and pension experts based in the United States. We obtained broad perspectives on the benefits and drawbacks of the countries' regulatory oversight activities and the identified key strategies. Where possible, we attempted to obtain basic demographic data and available data on the types and amounts of fees paid in DC plans in those countries from government officials, pension experts, and others we interviewed. We used these data for the purpose of providing background information and context, or examples, of the effect of certain strategies on fees. We performed some basic reasonableness checks of the data against other sources of information. We did not compare fees across countries because each country, and sometimes plans within a country, can charge different fees; instead, we looked at the types and amounts of fees in each country to gain a better understanding of the effect of key strategies used to lower fees. We did not conduct an independent legal analysis to verify the information provided by or about the laws or regulations of the foreign countries selected for this study. Instead, we relied on appropriate secondary sources and interviews to support our work. Following our interviews, we submitted key statements of facts for review and verification by agency officials in each country and incorporated technical corrections as necessary.

We conducted this performance audit from March 2011 through March 2012 in accordance with generally accepted government auditing standards. Those standards require that we plan and perform the audit to obtain sufficient, appropriate evidence to provide a reasonable basis for our findings and conclusions based on our audit objectives. We believe that the evidence obtained provides a reasonable basis for our findings and conclusions based on our audit objectives.

APPENDIX II. KEY FEATURES OF DC PENSION SYSTEMS IN AUSTRALIA, CHILE, SWEDEN AND THE UNITED KINGDOM

Australia

At a Glance

Since 1992, Australia has had a mandatory pension system, known as superannuation.

Total system assets: Pension assets totaled about $1.04 trillion USD in 2010, of which approximately 82 percent were in defined contribution (DC) plans.

Coverage: Employers are required to offer a pension plan to eligible workers and provide a minimum level of contributions. The plan may be defined benefit (DB) or DC, but the majority of plans are DC.[50]

Types of Plans in the System

Industry-wide or single-employer (28% of private plan assets) The plan is a nonprofit entity managed by a board of trustees, some of which must have equal representation from employers and participants. Trustees must be licensed by the government and are subject to a "fit and proper" test, which specifies certain standards, including experience and educational and technical qualifications.

Retail (34% of private plan assets) A participant deals directly with a for-profit service provider which manages their account. Within the service provider, the plan is managed by a board of trustees. Similar to industry-wide and single-employer plans, trustees must be licensed and are subject to a "fit and proper" test.

Self-managed (38% of private plan assets) A participant manages his/her own account, which entails establishing a trust and a bank account. Up to four people can be in a trust. The participant is the trustee and can select investment options.

Source: GAO analysis of foreign agency documentation and interviews with Australian officials and industry experts.

Pension System Highlights

Contributions: The current minimum employer contribution rate is 9 percent of the worker's earnings. The government has proposed to increase this amount to 12 percent. The contribution is required for a band of earnings, which is capped at about 2.5 times average wages.[51] Employers and participants may also choose to make additional contributions subject to a cap.[52] Individuals can voluntarily make contributions when they are unemployed.

Investment options: Most plans offer participants a choice of investment options. On average, retail plans offer 219 investment options and industry funds offer 10 investment options. Participants can choose to receive investment advice for a fee from their plan or from an external advisor. According to agency officials, one-on-one advice can entail high fees and few participants use it.

Default option: Since 2005, employers have been required to designate a default plan for those participants who do not specify in which plan they want their contributions deposited. Australia is in the process of implementing a new set of standards for the default investment option, known as MySuper. Under MySuper, all default investment options must be approved by the pensions regulator and meet standards for diversification and fees. In addition, the default investment options must be unbundled from additional services, such as investment advice.

Leakage: Participants are generally not allowed to access their accounts prior to age 55. When workers change jobs they may leave their account at their previous plan or roll it over into a new plan. As part of the recommendations made from a 2010 review of the superannuation system, Australia is considering implementing a process called "auto consolidation," which would match a worker who is starting a new job to any pre-existing superannuation accounts they may already have.

Drawdown: The minimum age to begin drawing down benefits is currently 55, set to increase to 60 by 2025. The accumulated benefit can be withdrawn as a lump-sum or as an annuity. Most benefits are taken as a lump-sum. Participants over age 55 who are still working may start drawing down benefits. Employers are required to continue to contribute to a worker's fund until the worker reaches age 70, or the worker retires or separates from the employer.

Chile

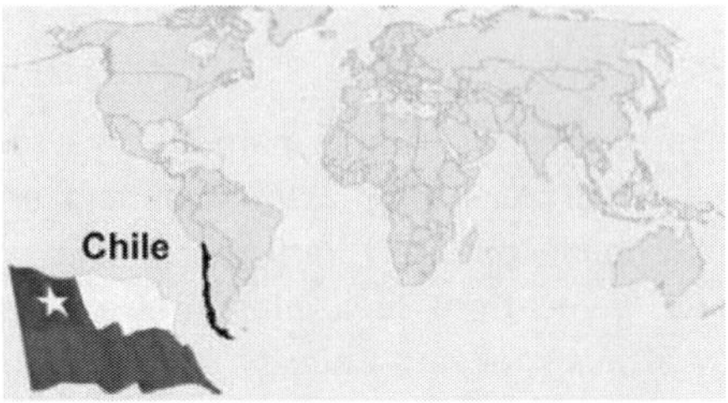

At a Glance

Chile replaced its DB public pension system with individual accounts in 1981. Workers who entered the labor market after that date are mandated to join an individual DC account.[53]

Total system assets: The value of pension assets totaled $148.4 billion USD in 2010, according to the pensions regulator.

Coverage: Workers are required to contribute to an individual DC account. About 60 percent of those employed participate in the system.[54]

Type of Plan in the System

Workers can choose which licensed for-profit service provider, known as an AFP (*Administradoras de Fondos de Pensiones*), manages their individual accounts. Currently, there are six AFPs. New entrants to the labor force are defaulted to the AFP with the lowest fee as determined by a bidding process, which takes place every 2 years.

Source: GAO analysis of foreign agency documentation and interviews with Chilean officials and industry experts.

Pension System Highlights

Contributions: Workers are required to contribute 10 percent of applicable earnings to their individual account—the earnings ceiling is equal to 67.4 indexed units (*Unidades de Fomento*) of accounts that are equivalent to about 1,500,000 Chilean pesos, or $2,900 USD a month as of December 2011. In addition to their contribution, participants pay fees to their AFP, which currently range from 1.14 percent to 2.36 percent of earnings.[55]

Investment options: Workers can choose between five types of funds, labeled A through E (in descending order of investment risk), offered by each AFP.[56] Each category of funds is subject to limits on the amount of equities that may be held corresponding to its risk level. Participants are subject to restrictions on which investment funds they may hold based on their age. The 2008 reforms created the figure of the pension advisor, a professional who will be able to advise individuals on a range of issues, including the choice of AFP and investment and drawdown options.[57]

Default option: For those who do not choose an investment option within an AFP, the default option is a lifecycle investment strategy in which allocations to risky funds decrease with age (e.g., B fund for workers under 35, C fund for men between 36 and 55 and women between 36 and 50, and D fund for men above 55 and women above 50). According to officials, about 25 percent of workers make an active choice.

Leakage: Early retirement is permitted at any age provided the accumulated capital can finance a pension above a certain threshold. Otherwise, workers do not have access to their account balance before normal retirement age, which is 65 for men and 60 for women.

Drawdown: Upon retirement, participants may choose one of two major options: (a) buy an annuity from an insurance company that pays lifetime benefits; or (b) set up programmed withdrawals with an AFP. Variations on these two options include purchasing a deferred annuity, which means setting a future date for purchasing an annuity and, until that date, making programmed withdrawals from the individual account; or purchasing an immediate annuity with a portion of the funds in the individual account and making programmed withdrawals with the rest of the funds.[58]

Sweden

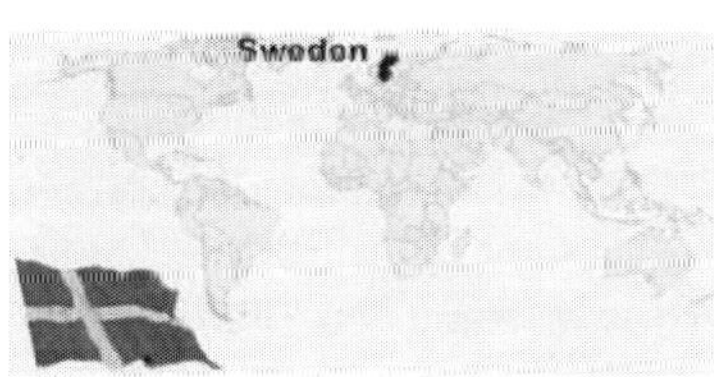

At a Glance

In the mid-1990s, Sweden reformed its mandatory, earnings-related public pension scheme and added a system of individual accounts, called the Premium Pension system.

Total system assets: According to officials, Premium Pension assets totaled approximately $62 billion USD in 2010.

Coverage: Workers and their employers are required to contribute a portion of the workers' salaries to individual DC accounts.[59] Self-employed workers are also required to contribute a portion of their salaries to individual DC accounts.

Type of Plan in the System

A government agency, the Swedish Pensions Agency, administers the DC plan and handles recordkeeping for all accounts. Any fund provider licensed in Sweden or registered in their own country can offer funds in the Premium Pension system as long as they agree to certain conditions set by the Swedish Pensions Agency, including a set rebate schedule for all funds, based on the funds' total assets in the Premium Pension system.

Source: GAO analysis of foreign agency documentation and interviews with Swedish officials and industry experts.

Pension System Highlights

Contributions: Employers and workers are required to contribute 2.5 percent of the covered portion of a worker's salary. In 2011, the ceiling for contributions was approximately $1,400 USD. Contributions are collected from employers by the national tax authority on a monthly basis.

Investment options: Participants can choose up to five funds from among nearly 800 different funds—at the end of 2010 there were 789 funds administered by 94 different fund management companies and the default fund provider.[60] The Swedish Pensions Agency is currently developing a fund selection tool to help participants make fund decisions depending on, among other things, their desired investment risk. Participants can choose to receive investment advice for a fee from external advisers. According to government and industry officials, because of the large number of investment options, participants are increasingly using these advice services but it can be expensive and undermine the low-cost design of the system.

Default option: For those participants who do not select specific funds, their contributions are placed in a default option called the Seventh AP Fund (AP7 Såfa). AP7 is an independent, government entity operated as a nonprofit with a board of directors appointed by the Swedish government. Since May 2010, AP7 Såfa defaults participants under the age of 56 into global equity funds and shifts the accounts for those ages 56 and older by 3 to 4 percent per year into bonds to reduce investment risk.[61]

Leakage: Participants are not allowed to access their Premium Pension accounts prior to age 61.

Drawdown: At retirement, participants are required to annuitize their retirement savings and the Swedish Pensions Agency acts as the annuity provider for the Premium Pension system. When participants annuitize their benefit, they can choose among two options:

- variable annuity—participants' holdings remain invested in their chosen funds and the Swedish Pensions Agency pays their benefits from those funds,[62] or

- with profit annuity—participants' holdings are sold and moved into an insurance product that pays at least a set amount per year.[63]

United Kingdom

At a Glance

Voluntary DC plans make up most of the private pension system in the U.K. An individual may be a member of a number of different pension plans simultaneously. From 2012 to 2017, all employers will be required to automatically enroll eligible employees into a pension plan—including a new low-cost DC pension savings plan called the National Employment Savings Trust (NEST)—and provide a minimum contribution.

Total system assets: According to officials, pension assets totaled approximately $3.3 trillion USD in 2010, of which approximately 40 percent were in DC plans.

Coverage: Individuals in the U.K. can voluntarily contribute to pension arrangements that can be employer-sponsored (DB or DC) or individually arranged (DC). These arrangements are utilized by about half of the working age population, and of those workers only about 30 percent of participants are members of DC plans, including public and private pensions.

Types of Plans in the System

Trust-based plans (45% of DC participants) These are employer-sponsored plans and are usually nonprofit entities managed by a board of trustees that typically hire one or more service providers for recordkeeping and investment management services. The trustees are responsible for selecting and vetting the investment options.

Contract-based plans (55% of DC participants) For contract-based plans, an employee deals directly with a for-profit service provider which performs both recordkeeping and investment management services.[64] The service provider selects which investment options are available to the participant. These plans are owned entirely by the worker.

Source: GAO analysis of foreign agency documentation and interviews with U.K. officials and industry experts.

Pension System Highlights

Contributions: Employers and workers may make contributions to DC plans. While employers have not previously been required to make any contributions, beginning in 2012, they will be required to automatically enroll eligible workers into a pension plan and provide a minimum contribution.

Workers will have the right to opt-out of the plan.[65] The minimum total contribution of 8 percent of qualifying earnings will be contributed to the selected private pension—4 percent will usually be contributed by employees, which is usually matched by a compulsory 3 percent from the employer and a minimum 1 percent from the government, delivered through tax relief.[66]

Investment options: DC plans typically offer between 5 and 10 investment options, but contract-based plans may offer far more than trust-based plans. According to a U.K. service provider, approximately 70 percent of DC assets in the U.K. are in passively managed funds. To choose between the options available to them, participants can receive investment advice from an external advisor.

Default option: When a default investment option is offered to participants within a DC plan, it was estimated in 2009 that 81 percent of members invested in it. All plans used by employers to satisfy their duties for auto-enrollment will be required to have a default fund.

Leakage: Currently, individuals cannot access their private pension savings until they reach the minimum pension age (age 55 as of April 2010).

Drawdown: When employer plans allow it, individuals can continue working while receiving pension benefits. While participants were previously required to annuitize their pension benefits by age 75, as of April 2011, participants over age 55 can now withdraw their pension savings by choosing one or a combination of the following options:

- purchasing an annuity;
- investing their funds in a Capped Drawdown account, which allows them to withdraw up to 100 percent of the value of an equivalent annuity as an income from their pension fund while leaving the remaining fund invested;
- withdrawing their funds flexibly provided that individuals can demonstrate a secured guaranteed lifetime income of at least approximately $31,600 USD per year; or
- withdrawing their funds as a lump-sum when their accumulated balance is very small.

End Notes

[1] Reasonable Contract or Arrangement Under Section 408(b)(2) - Fee Disclosure, 77 Fed. Reg. 5632 (2012) (to be codified at 29 C.F.R. pt. 2550).

[2] Employee Benefit Research Institute, *Employment-Based Retirement Plan Participation: Geographic Differences and Trends, 2010*, Issue Brief No. 363 (Washington D.C.: October 2011).

[3] Employee Benefit Research Institute, *401(k) Plan Asset Allocation, Account Balances, and Loan Activity in 2010*, Issue Brief No. 366 (Washington D.C.: December 2011).

[4] Exemptions to this trust requirement include insurance contracts and plan assets held by insurance companies.

[5] 29 U.S.C. §1104(a). The law establishes that a plan fiduciary includes a person who has discretionary control or authority over the management or administration of the plan, including the plan's assets. Typically, the plan sponsor is a fiduciary under this definition. ERISA requires that plan fiduciaries carry out their responsibilities prudently and do so solely in the interest of the plan's participants and beneficiaries. In accordance with ERISA and related Labor regulations and guidance, plan sponsors and other fiduciaries must exercise an appropriate level of care and diligence given the scope of the plan and act for the exclusive benefit of plan participants and beneficiaries, rather than for their own or another party's gain.

[6] We have previously reported that plan sponsors may still pay some plan recordkeeping fees but participants bear them in a growing number of plans. GAO, *Private Pensions: Changes Needed to Provide 401(k) Plan Participants and the Department of Labor Better Information on Fees*, GAO-07-21 (Washington, D.C.: Nov.16, 2006).

[7] The Employee Benefits Security Administration (EBSA) also has oversight responsibilities related to other types of DC plans, as well as DB plans. The Internal Revenue Service also oversees various aspects of 401(k) contributions under the Internal Revenue Code.

[8] 29 U.S.C. § 1002(21)(A). On October 22, 2010, Labor proposed a revised definition of the term "fiduciary," 75 Fed. Reg. 65,263 (2010) and, subsequently, by News Release Number: 11-1382-NAT on September 19, 2011, Labor announced it would "re-propose" its rule on the definition of fiduciary in early 2012.

[9] GAO, *401(K) Plans: Improved Regulation Could Better Protect Participants from Conflicts of Interest*, GAO-11-119 (Washington, D.C.: Jan. 28, 2011) and *Defined Benefit Pensions: Conflicts of Interest Involving High Risk or Terminated Plans Pose Enforcement Challenges*, GAO-07-703 (Washington, D.C.: June 28, 2007).

[10] GAO, *Employee Benefits Security Administration: Enforcement Improvements Made but Additional Actions Could Further Enhance Pension Plan Oversight*, GAO-07-22 (Washington, D.C.: Jan. 18, 2007).

[11] An annuity is an insurance agreement or contract that comes in a number of different forms and can (1) help individuals accumulate money for retirement through tax-deferred savings, (2) provide them with monthly income that can be guaranteed to last for as long as they live, or (3) do both. Payments from fixed annuities are generally a set regular amount, whereas payments from variable annuities may increase or decrease based on performance of the underlying investments.

[12] Fiduciary Requirements for Disclosure in Participant-Directed Individual Account Plans; Final Rule, 75 Fed. Reg. 64,910 (October 20, 2010) (codified at 29 C.F.R. § 2550.404a-5). A revised and delayed effective date for this regulation was published on July 19, 2011 (76 Fed. Reg. 42539).

[13] While the Organisation for Economic Co-operation and Development (OECD) recently acknowledged Chile's efforts to develop its market-based economy, it generally is understood to have more moderate social welfare policies than the United States. and publicly spends less on social welfare as a percentage of its GDP. Australia is also generally

considered a market-based economy, but is understood to offer similar social welfare provisions to that of the U.S. and publicly spends about the same on social welfare as a percentage of its GDP.

[14] GDP per capita is based on purchasing power parity, which equalizes the purchasing power of different currencies in their home countries by taking into account the relative cost of living and the inflation rates of different countries, rather than just a nominal GDP comparison.

[15] Plans must also register with the tax authority in order to obtain tax benefits.

[16] Guidelines provided by the International Organisation of Pension Supervisors (IOPS) specify that risk-based pension supervision should be evaluative, data driven, and forward-looking. IOPS, *Toolkit for Risk-based Pensions Supervision: Introduction to Risk-based Pensions Supervision* (2011). According to an IOPS working paper, the main risks in DC pension systems are those that impact the accumulated pension savings of participants and therefore the amount of pension benefit participants receive in retirement. They include investment risk; high costs, such as excessive fees; operating risks, such as administrating individual accounts; and managing the transition from accumulation to decumulation. John Ashcroft and Fiona Stewart, *Managing and Supervising Risks in Defined Contribution Pension Systems,* IOPS Working Paper No. 12 (October 2010).

[17] IOPS is an independent international body with 70 members and observers representing about 60 countries and territories. Its purpose is, among other things, to serve as the standard-setting body on pension supervision and regulation; to promote international cooperation; to provide a worldwide forum for policy dialogue and exchange of information on pension supervision; and to participate in the work of relevant international bodies in the area of pensions.

[18] According to Labor, the Paperwork Reduction Act inhibits EBSA's ability to similarly collect information.

[19] In October 2002, the Australian pensions regulator first introduced risk assessment and supervisory response tools that formed the centerpiece of its risk-based approach.

[20] When the Australian pensions regulator identifies a superannuation plan that it considers too small, it initiates conversations with the plan trustees suggesting merger opportunities. Such mergers are eligible for tax relief.

[21] The adoption of a risk-based approach in Chile followed an initial assessment by the World Bank and The Financial Sector Assessment Program. It was also recommended by the OECD during Chile's accession to the organization.

[22] Active communication could include issuing guidance to regulated pension plans explaining requirements and good practices, ensuring that communication with regulated pension plans is ongoing, and working closely with industry professionals such as accountants and actuaries, which can help regulated pension plans apply standards.

[23] GAO and GAO-11-119 . In addition, Labor's enforcement efforts regarding potential conflicts of interest related to investment advice have not addressed potential violations by non-ERISA fiduciary service providers. This applies to Labor's civil investigations. However, according to Labor, for its criminal investigations the subject need not be an ERISA fiduciary because an allegation of fraud is sufficient to trigger Labor's jurisdiction.

[24] The U.K. pensions regulator is currently in the process of developing a new regulatory framework for DC plans which will be based on a segmented approach (e.g., larger plans tend to be better run and achieve economies of scale, whereas smaller plans are more likely to have lower governance standards and higher charges).

[25] These officials also noted that the enhanced disclosures may not capture all fees, like transaction costs, and government and industry surveys have shown that some participants do not read the disclosures. Swedish Pensions Agency, *Surveys About The Orange Envelope of 2011* (Stockholm, Sweden: April 2011). Social Protection Surveys have been conducted in Chile since 2002 and the last available year is 2009. In addition, the Chilean pensions regulator conducts focus groups.

[26] John A. Turner and Hazel A. Witte, *Fee Disclosure to Pension Participants: Establishing Minimum Requirements*, International Centre for Pension Management Sponsored Research, Joseph L. Rotman School of Management, University of Toronto (Toronto, Canada: August 2008).

[27] Fees for external fund management that are deducted from the external funds to determine the fund's performance are not included in this total, but the Chilean pensions regulator requires plan providers to report these fees to the regulator and publishes this information online on a regular basis.

[28] Because the Swedish Pensions Agency charges one administrative charge for all participants, the fund management fee is the pertinent fee for comparison purposes.

[29] Self-managed superannuation funds require a lower level of disclosure, but are still subject to some of the same disclosure requirements as other superannuation plans.

[30] Transaction fees, however, are directly deducted from the fund returns and reported in aggregate in the Swedish Pensions Agency's annual report.

[31] Because of the small number of plans available to Chilean participants, this type of disclosure is likely clearer than it would be if participants were offered many more choices.

[32] According to a February 2011 survey conducted by AARP, 71 percent of plan participants thought they paid no 401(k) fees, while only 23 percent knew they paid fees. In addition, the survey found that 62 percent were unaware of how much they paid in fees for their plan and 32 percent did not feel knowledgeable about the impact that fees could have on their retirement savings. AARP, *401(k) Participants' Awareness and Understanding of Fees* (Washington, D.C.: February 2011).

[33] In comparison, the amount of fees a DC plan participant pays in the U.S. can vary considerably across plans. As we previously reported, U.S. participants tend to pay the same types of fees (e.g. investment management and recordkeeping fees), but the amount of those fees depends on a number of factors, which could be related to the employer's size and actions it takes as a plan sponsor. For example, sponsors may decrease fees by combining or pooling assets to access certain investment products or negotiate with service providers. However, U.S. workers are limited to the plans offered by their employers and some of those plans charge higher fees than others. GAO, *Retirement Savings: Better Information and Sponsor Guidance Could Improve Oversight and Reduce Fees for Participants*, GAO-09-641 (Washington, D.C.: Sept. 4, 2009).

[34] Sweden's Premium Pension system represents the only traditional DC portion of the public DC system. The U.K.'s NEST is a nationally available plan, implemented along with the U.K.'s auto-enrollment requirements, in order to provide all employers a low-cost plan in which to enroll their employees. NEST's trustee body has a public service obligation to accept any employer who wishes to offer the plan to its employees.

[35] According to the Swedish Pensions Agency, fund providers for the Swedish system are required to rebate from about 55 to 81 percent of their retail fee based on the type of funds they offer (equity or bond) and their aggregate market share in the system. Providers send rebates to the administrative body every 3 months, although it distributes rebates to affected participants in the following year.

[36] Administrative fees in Sweden have fallen from 0.30 to 0.16 percent between 2001 and 2011. Swedish officials expect to continually lower administrative fees because the system's assets will continue to grow, and since administrative costs are typically fixed, they will decline per participant as the system's assets grow. Sweden charges fees for fund management separate from administrative fees, and these fees in January 2012 ranged from 0 to 2.57 percent.

[37] Turner and Witte (2008) and Tapia, W. and J. Yermo (2008), "Fees in Individual Account Pension Systems: A Cross-Country Comparison", *OECD Working Papers on Insurance and Private Pensions*, No. 27, OECD publishing, © OECD. doi:10.1787/236114516708.

[38] While the U.K. designed this nationally available plan to be low-cost, decisions about the plan are made by a trustee body. The original members of the body were appointed by the

government. The choice of future NEST trustee members will be made by the NEST trustee body and the representative member panel will participate in the recruitment and appointment of NEST's trustee members.

[39] The plan also received a loan from the British government that will allow them to spread startup costs over a certain amount of time for which the plan will charge participants an additional 1.8 percent of contributions until the loan is paid off. Officials' calculations indicate that the total effective charge on participants will be about 0.50 percent per year, based on the average participant. The officials stated that they expect the loan to be repaid in about 20 years.

[40] *Super System Review: Review of the Governance, Efficiency, Structure and Operation of Australia's Superannuation System* (Commonwealth of Australia, June 30, 2010).

[41] In 2010, the investment strategy for the default fund, AP7 Såfa, was updated to take a higher-risk, age-adapted approach since an increasing number of participants were choosing the default option—96 percent of new entrants in 2010, according to a default fund official—and many of those participants were young adults. AP7 Såfa also now offers different risk-level funds ("offensive," "balanced," and "cautious") that do not change based on a participant's age.

[42] The second bidding process finished in February 2012 and the AFP that won will charge 0.77 percent of salary for the 2 years starting August 2012.

[43] Fee amounts are effective as of March 2012. Participants paying fees as a percent of salary pay more upfront as a percent of their account balance than participants paying asset-based fees, which have a much smoother effect over time. Fees as a percent of salary in Chile are deducted as an additional amount of a participant's salary—Chilean employers are required to remit to a Chilean plan provider (1) 10 percent of a worker's salary as a contribution and, (2) on top of that contribution, an additional percent of salary according to the provider's fee. For example, if a participant contributed to a provider that charged a 1.48 percent fee, their employer would remit 11.48 percent of their salary (10 percent contribution plus 1.48 percent fee) to the provider on the participant's behalf. While this fee represents a large portion of participants' account balances in early years, it represents less of their account balances in later years. Over a participant's lifetime, this fee could translate into an approximately 0.58 percent asset-based fee at present values.

[44] If the requirements are finalized, an Australian government release states that, from October 1, 2013, employers must make contributions for workers who have not chosen their fund, to a fund offering a MySuper product in order to satisfy superannuation guarantee obligations, and by July 1, 2017, funds will need to transfer the existing default balances of workers to a MySuper product.

[45] Officials note that funds will be able to offer a discounted administration fee to workers of particular employers. Funds will also have the flexibility to offer employers with more than 500 workers a MySuper product tailored to the needs of the particular workplace. To maintain transparency of these arrangements, the details of all separately tailored MySuper products and discounted administration fees will be required to be reported to the pensions regulator and will also need to be separately published by trustees.

[46] Trustees wanting to offer a MySuper product will be required to apply to the pensions regulator to be authorized for each MySuper product.

[47] Chile also caps fees for certain drawdown products and fees that service providers can pay to external managers for retail class shares, which have both helped to bring fees down.

[48] Officials noted that legislation requiring advisors to compare plans offered by for-profit providers to these low-cost plans with the explicit fee cap may have helped to lower fees.

[49] Requirements of the trustee board as a whole included that they have appropriate knowledge, manage conflicts of interest, and have a policy regarding oversight of service providers.

[50] The Australian pensions regulator reports that, as of June 2010, 17.6 percent of superannuation assets for entities with more than four members were in DB plans.

[51] Employers are not required to contribute for workers earning less than about $500 USD a month.

[52] According to the Australian Tax Office, there is a cap of about $25,600 USD per year on tax deductible contributions for participants up to age 50. For participants age 50 and above, the cap is about $51,100 USD.

[53] Additional reforms in 2008 added a Basic Solidarity Pension for individuals with no pensions and a Solidarity Pension Payment for those with low pensions, both targeted to the poorest 60 percent of the population.

[54] This is partly due to the fact that the self-employed (about 25 percent of total employment) were not required to contribute and voluntary contributions for this group have been historically low. The 2008 Pension Reform determines that contribution for self-employed workers is mandatory. The introduction of the obligation will be gradual. During the period 2012 to 2014, the default option will be to contribute with the option to opt-out. It will be mandatory for self-employed workers to contribute from 2015 onward.

[55] Each participant also pays a fee for disability and survivorship insurance, which is currently 1.49 percent of earnings.

[56] Initially, only one type of fund was permitted to be offered by an AFP, which was invested in equities and fixed income (current C fund). Since 2000, four additional types of funds have been permitted, ranging from a fixed income fund (E Fund) to an aggressive equity fund (A Fund).

[57] Until recently, plan participants and retirees could get advice from their AFPs or insurance and annuity brokers, but the pensions regulator recognized that this advice may not be considered impartial and objective. Under the current regulations, the names of pension advisors appear in a joint register kept by the pensions and securities regulators, both of which are also responsible for overseeing several aspects of their services. Pension advisors' fees are subject to a ceiling.

[58] For all these pension options, if the worker obtains a pension higher than 150 percent of the minimum pension guaranteed by the state and higher than 70 percent of his/her average monthly taxable wage for the previous 10 years, he/she may use of the sum of money remaining in the individual account as desired (after the calculation of the amount needed to obtain the pension has been made and this has been deducted from the accumulated balance).

[59] Employers are also required to contribute to an Income Pension (notional DC) for each worker and may also contribute to supplementary Occupational Pensions (which can be DC or DB plans), but for the purpose of this report we focused on the Premium Pension system.

[60] The default fund provider allows participants to opt into and out of some funds they offer, which are based on risk-levels (cautious, balanced, and offensive).

[61] According to a default fund representative, this high-risk approach was chosen because of the low percentage of participants' overall pension invested in the Premium Pension system.

[62] These annuities do not have a guaranteed value. To calculate the pension for these annuities, the Swedish Pensions Agency divides the value of the account by an annuity divisor (based on estimated average life expectancy) and credits the outcome with an estimated future interest rate minus administrative costs. The Swedish Pensions Agency recalculates the pension amount each year to reflect developments in the value of the participants' chosen funds. For example, if returns in participants' chosen funds exceed the estimated future interest rate, then, generally, the participants' annual pension amount is increased.

[63] However, the participants' annual pension amount may increase above the set amount in any given year.

[64] Some service providers outsource one or both of these services. Contract-based schemes are owned entirely by the employee, but may be facilitated by the employer. If they are facilitated by the employer, some employers appoint a committee to oversee the service providers' arrangements.

[65] This is the requirement provided that the employee's earnings are above the current proposed auto-enrollment threshold of about $11,800 USD. Employees with earnings below this level will be permitted to opt in to the scheme. There will be a contribution limit of about $6,800 USD a year into NEST.

[66] Qualifying earnings represent the portion of a worker's salary over about $9,000 USD and below about $60,400 USD (as of February 2012). For the first 5 years of auto-enrollment implementation (from October 1, 2012, to September 30, 2017) the minimum total contribution is 2 percent and minimum employer contribution is 1 percent. For the year after that (October 1, 2017, to September 30, 2018) the minimum percentages move up to 5 and 2, respectively. From October 1, 2018, the full 8 percent and 3 percent apply.

In: 401(k) Plans and Spend-Down Options ISBN: 978-1-63117-580-0
Editor: Erica L. Chapmann

Chapter 3

EXAMINING INCOME REPLACEMENT DURING RETIREMENT YEARS IN A DEFINED CONTRIBUTION PLAN SYSTEM*

Advisory Council on Employee Welfare and Pension Benefit Plans

ABSTRACT

The 2012 ERISA Advisory Council (the Council) examined income replacement during retirement years in a defined contribution retirement system and the issues individuals and plan sponsors face to ensure financial security during the participants' retirement years. In the past, the challenge of providing retired employees with a source of income to last during their retirement was primarily met through a source of lifetime income provided by employer-sponsored defined benefit pension (DB) plans. To that end, DB plans typically offered an annuitized benefit to participants. The responsibility of providing such a lifetime benefit was that of the plan sponsor through the design of the plan. However, the continued shift from DB plans to defined contribution (DC) plans as a primary source of retirement income has shifted the burden of providing a continued stream of income during the retirement years of DC plan participants. As a result of this shift there is a growing need for plan sponsors to examine, evaluate and make available to participants, options designed to address their retirement income needs in a DC plan context.

* This is an edited, reformatted and augmented version of a report dated December 2012.

In addition, there is a need to sufficiently educate participants so that they can fully understand the importance of viewing and analyzing their account balances as a source of lifetime income. The Council believes that this education will better equip participants to exercise meaningful choices with regards to their continued financial security during retirement.

The purpose of the Council's examination of this issue is to provide recommendations to the Department of Labor (DOL) on guidance for plan sponsors and participants at a time that this topic is being highlighted among pension experts, and the market is beginning to respond with innovative products. Examination of the issue focused on the following: (1) the challenges participants face in making their account balances last for the length of their retirement years, especially in light of improved longevity; (2) what options and resources should be available to participants to help them in their efforts to transform their accumulated savings into a continued flow of income designed to last over their retirement lives and/or the lives of their spouses; (3) what considerations and/or challenges plan sponsors encounter when making these options available to plan participants; and (4) what considerations and challenges face plan sponsors in providing education outreach for participants of DC plans regarding available income replacement options.

Through testimony and research, the Council developed recommendations to the Secretary that certain plan sponsors and participants may find beneficial when examining options for income replacement in a DC plan system. Specifically, the recommendations in this report include enhancing regulatory and sub-regulatory guidance that may help plan sponsors address their fiduciary concerns when offering income replacement options or advice on available options, and the development of educational/outreach materials for both plan sponsors and participants to result in a greater chance of DC participants achieving lifetime income in retirement.

ACKNOWLEDGMENTS

The Council recognizes the following individuals and organizations who contributed greatly to the Council's deliberations and final report.

Larry Good	Employee Benefits Security Administration (EBSA)
DiWeena Streater	EBSA

June 13, 2012

Jeffrey Turner	EBSA

Olivia Mitchell	Pension Research Council of the Wharton School
Bruce Ashton	Drinker Biddle & Reith, LLP
Michael Hadley	Davis & Harmon, LLP
Abigail Pancoast	Lincoln Financial Group, for American Council of Life Insurers (ACLI)
Kelli Hueler	Hueler Companies
Allison Klausner	Honeywell International, for American Benefits Council (ABC)
Kevin T. Hanney	United Technologies Corporation

August 30, 2012

Cynthia Mallett	MetLife
Richard Pretty	TIAA-CREF
Sri Reddy	Prudential Financial
Richard Bailey	VALIC
Jason Scott	Financial Engines
Stephen Sexauer	Allianz Global Investments
Julie McPeak	Tennessee Department of Commerce and Insurance, for NAIC

I. Executive Summary

Traditionally, defined benefit plans (DB) offered participants a steady stream of income through their retirement years as a result of plan design and distribution options. With the continued shift from DB plans to defined contribution plans (DC) as a primary source of retirement income there is a growing need to examine options designed to respond to participants' retirement security needs, and the inherent risks of either outliving their income or not being able to maintain a certain lifestyle during retirement.

Some of the issues discussed in this report include:

- Whether a plan should focus on providing a single benefit option or multiple benefit options in an effort to adequately address the different needs of participants, including diversification;
- The factors to be considered by the plan sponsor in making income replacement options available;

- Whether there are additional fiduciary considerations raised by making various options available, and how plans sponsors/plan administrators prudently manage these issues while adequately assisting plan participants;
- What are the challenges participants face in making their account balances in DC plans last for the length of their retirement years, especially in light of improved longevity;
- What are some of the lifetime income replacement options available to participants that would help them in their efforts to make their accumulated savings last over their retirement lives and/or the lives of their spouses;
- What level of education should be provided to plan sponsors and participants to assist them in evaluating and selecting lifetime income replacement options.

The Council researched and took testimony on (1) the challenges participants face in making their account balances last throughout their retirement years, and (2) what options would be helpful in their efforts to make their accumulated savings last over their retirement lives and/or the lives of their spouses. With respect to the participants, the Council received testimony and reviewed materials involving the type of educational materials that should be made available for participants to assist them in evaluating and selecting income replacement options.

The Council also received testimony on the challenges plan sponsors encounter when offering certain income replacement options, as well as providing education regarding the spend-down options of the participant's account balances. In particular, witnesses discussed the current concerns with respect to fiduciary liability that could be triggered when providing education to participants that goes beyond the "accumulation of assets" phase. In addition, there was much discussion that focused on the standard that must be upheld by sponsors when selecting an annuity issuer as set forth in DOL Regulation section 2550.401a-4.

Witnesses that appeared before the Council include members of the Employee Benefits Security Administration (DOL), representatives from the National Association of Insurance Commissioners (NAIC), investment managers and investment advisors, and attorneys that counsel plan sponsors on the administration of pension and welfare benefit funds.

II. RECOMMENDATIONS

After examining the issue of Income Replacement During Retirement Years in a Defined Contribution Plan System, the Council developed the following recommendations. The Council recommends that:

1. DOL review, modify, and/or develop regulatory guidance/clarification with respect to decumulation of retirement assets, including a defined contribution plan annuity safe harbor, participant education, and investment advice. The guidance/clarification should be designed to reduce current barriers faced by fiduciaries, plan sponsors, and service providers in their efforts to encourage participants to develop post-retirement income strategies and to consider alternatives in offering income replacement options.
2. DOL develop more immediate clarification in the same areas in the form of FAQs or other sub-regulatory guidance while DOL examines the recommendation set forth above.
3. DOL develop educational materials to assist employers and plan sponsors in evaluating and selecting income replacement options. The materials should focus on aspects such as:
   a) The need to accomplish a shift in the perception of defined contribution plans, to include the importance of the decumulation (retirement distribution) process;
   b) Commonly applied definitions;
   c) Features, designs, risks, and trade-offs;
   d) Roles of a plan sponsor/employer when offering income replacement options, education, and advice;
   e) Review and evaluation of projection tools used for income replacement stream;
   f) Lessons from behavioral finance and research about misconceptions related to income strategies, planning horizons, and understanding of longevity risks
4. DOL develop educational materials to assist individuals in understanding and choosing income replacement options to best suit their retirement needs, including:
   a) The importance of understanding the life-cycle approach to planning,
   b) Key features, designs, risks, and trade-offs;

c) The importance of understanding the tools and assumptions used to project income stream;
d) The need to evaluate all household sources of retirement income, including survivor benefits and Social Security;
e) The impact of inflation and inflation assumptions;
f) Understanding the impact of longevity and longevity risk, the need for a long planning horizon and potential benefits from mortality risk pooling;
g) The timing of decisions and alternatives.

Other Important Issues

A. Auto enrollment or other default features for income replacement options which could include a safe harbor.
B. Barriers to a plan sponsor acting as a facilitator of income replacement options outside of an employer-sponsored plan.
C. Income illustrations of the participants' account balances on their benefit statements.

III. Background

1. The Shift in Retirement Coverage and Some Resulting Consequences

Employer-sponsored pensions represent an important component of retirement income. Since the early 1980s, the percentage of workers participating in a pension plan has remained around 50 percent of the private sector work force. However, in recent years pension coverage has seen a noticeable shift away from "traditional" DB plans to DC plans. According to recent reports, in the context of private employers offering DB single-employer pension plans, the percentage has decreased to less than 9 percent, while employers offering single-employer DC pension plan increased to more than 88 percent.

In traditional DB plans, workers typically accrue benefits that are based on years of service and earnings. In DC plans, participants have an individual account within the plan and the balance is a combination of a participant's contributions, investment gains or losses, and in some cases employer-matching contributions. One of the important differences between a DB plan and a DC plan is the method of distribution of the participant's benefit –in the DB plan the option of taking the accrued benefits in the form of a lifetime annuity is often presented to the participant.

In a DC plan this distribution option is generally the exception rather than the norm, with most account balances being distributed as a lump sum amount.

The continued trend toward expanding coverage under DC plans within our retirement system, and the corresponding shrinking coverage under DB plans, is producing a large percentage of workers who will be forced to rely increasingly on their DC plan accumulated account balances to provide financial security during their retirement years.

As the number of employees in this situation grows, these individuals will face having to make important decisions regarding how to make their account balances last for a desired length of time, and in many cases, last throughout their retirement years. Retirement years represent a period in life that is becoming increasingly longer due to improved longevity.

Longevity is used in this context to represent the number of years that is left for someone at a given age. Life expectancy in the United States has been on the rise for a decade, and in 2007 reached a high of nearly 78 years, up from 77.8 a year earlier.

Not only are people living longer, but they also are living an active lifestyle. In 2007, the average life expectancy for women was 80.4 years and 75.3 for men. The table below provides a summary of the recent life expectancy of individuals living in the United States:

Expectation of Life at Birth, 1970 to 2008, and Projections, 2010 to 2020

Years	Total	Males	Females
1970…..	70.8	67.1	74.7
1980-1982	74.5	70.8	78.1
1983-1985	74.7	71.1	78.2
1986-1988	74.9	71.4	78.3
1989-1991	75.5	72.0	78.9
1992-1994	75.7	72.4	78.0
1995-1997	76.5	73.6	79.4
1998-2000	76.8	74.1	79.3
2001-2003	77.1	74.5	79.8
2004-2006	77.7	75.1	80.2

(Continued)

Years	Total	Males	Females
2007-2008	78.0	75.5	80.5
Projections			
2010	78.3	75.7	80.8
2015	78.9	76.4	81.4
2020	79.5	77.1	81.9

Source: U.S. Census Bureau, Statistical Abstract of the United States: 2012.

The above table can even understate the impact of increased life expectancy on retirement income considerations. As people age, the average individual who survives to age 65 can be expected to live well beyond these general life expectancies set forth above. According to data provided by the Centers for Disease Control (http://www.cdc.gov/nchs/data/hus/2011/022.pdf) , while the average life expectancy from birth, in 2009, was 78.5, the average life expectancy for someone age 65 was 19.2 years, or age 84.2. The gap has narrowed somewhat from past years, as the absolute life expectancies have continued to increase. For example, the same data indicates that in 1980, while life expectancy at birth was 73.7 years, life expectancy for someone age 65 was 16.4 years, or age 81.4.

Increased life expectancy has resulted in some other issues that are important to retirement planning and individuals' efforts to have a financially secured retirement. These issues include the participants' appreciation of the impact of increased longevity on their financial security in retirement, participants' ability to understand and manage their retirement funds with declining age and cognitive ability, unexpected increased health care costs, and change in lifestyle in their retirement years. Some of the witnesses testified that there is a significant probability that retirement funds will need to last retirees as much as 30 years.

2. Evolving Market and Innovation for Income Replacement Options

Another aspect of this shift in retirement coverage is the growing need for employers who want to provide their workers with a secured retirement to examine and analyze lifetime income options designed to address their workers' retirement financial needs. In addition, there is the need for educational materials and outreach efforts that are designed to assist participants in understanding the importance of being able to convert their account balances into a steady stream of retirement income.

In responding to this need, some employers offer annuity distribution options, either through commercial annuities that are incorporated within the DC plan, or via transfers to a DB plan sponsored by the same employer as lifetime income distribution options. Another option is to provide the participant access to the account balance. In these cases, the participant can elect to withdraw the account balance where the account balance is paid either directly to the individual or rolled over to an Individual Retirement Account (IRA), or leave his/her account balance in the plan.

Often, when a participant elects to withdraw the account balance, in whole or by installments, this option is generally exercised without understanding the impact of this approach on whether the account balance will last throughout his/her retirement years. In some cases, a participant will elect to receive a lump sum distribution. In these cases, generally, little planning, if any, is done to ensure that the accumulated savings are transferred to an option designed to ensure that there is a stream of income paid over the participant's (or beneficiary's) retirement years.

In instances where the participant elects to leave the account balance in the plan, he/she can be faced with multiple options regarding how to improve his/her chances that the account balance will last for an elected period, including over his/her retirement years. These options can range from taking withdrawals (scheduled, unscheduled, or both) to annuitizing the account balance (partial or total; immediate or deferred; etc...), or additional alternatives that fall within the middle of this range. Generally, the availability of these options raises some important questions for fiduciaries and plan sponsors, including, but not limited to:

- Whether the plan should focus on providing a single option or multiple options in an effort to adequately address the different needs of participants, including diversification;
- The major factors to be considered by the plan sponsor in making these options available; and
- Whether there are additional fiduciary considerations raised by making various options available, and the prudent management of these issues while adequately assisting plan participants.

In the testimony presented to the Council, witnesses noted that the retirement product market is beginning to respond to the need for income replacement options within a DC retirement system. The witnesses stated that the market is still evolving and requested that any guidance provided by DOL be designed to allow for innovation in this area. Some of the products that are available in the market, and were discussed by the witnesses and Council members include:[1]

Traditional annuities. This product may be the most readily recognized because of the length of time it has been available (around for decades), and its exposure on the market (promoted both in and outside of plans). Under this product, the participant purchases the right from the insurer to receive monthly payments. The payments can be selected to be paid over the life of the participant and/or spouse, or for a selected period of time. Current payout rates under this product reflect the historically low interest rates and might average between 6-7 percent of the premium payment. Payout rates in higher interest rate environments can also be materially higher.

The major advantage of this product is that it can provide payments which are guaranteed for the lifetime of the participant. This is accomplished by pooling the risk that the participant will live beyond his or her life expectancy with the same risks for other individuals. The result is generally a lower cost to the participant, or alternatively a higher withdrawal than if he or she would have if solely responsible, on an individual basis, for making the assets last as long as the participant lived. To obtain this benefit, however, the participant generally must relinquish control over the funds at the point of purchase. Product variations that include some level of liquidity, however, also generally feature a higher cost.

Guaranteed minimum withdrawal benefits features. These products are often referred to as GMWBs, and represent a hybrid product with combined features. It generally consists of a mutual fund (such as a balanced or target date fund) or a similar investment product, and the guaranteed minimum withdrawal feature which is designed by the insurer. In exchange for premium payments, the insurer guarantees the participant payments that are equal to a percentage of the benefit base. The payments are initially made against the account balance and by the insurance company after the account is depleted. The payout rate can vary, but generally averages 5 percent (or 4.5 percent if there is joint life guarantee) of the investment amount. The guarantee is conditioned on the requirement that the participant not withdraw more than the specified amount per year. Withdrawals that exceed the stipulated amount will decrease the benefit base for determining future payments.

The major advantages of this product are (1) the flexibility for the participant to retain ownership of, and can access to, his/her investments and (2) the ability of the participant to pass any remaining cash value in the account to his/her heirs. The disadvantage is the requirement to adhere to a specified withdrawal annual amount which is generally less than payments under a traditional annuity.

Longevity insurance: this is an insurance product that is generally designed to begin payments when the participant reaches a specified age, often age 85. The insurance product can be combined with other retirement income approaches that are intended to address the income needs before the participant reaches the payout age under the insurance product.

The major advantage of this product is that the premiums are generally lower than other types of annuities. The disadvantage is that if the insured risk does not occur, i.e., the participant does not live to reach the stipulated age, the investment in the contract is lost.

Managed payout and retirement income mutual funds: these are typically mutual fund products (not insurance) and are designed to provide a steady stream of retirement income while allowing the participant access to the funds. Payments are made, generally monthly, at a specified rate that represents an average of 3-7 percent of the principal. There are two basic types of managed payout funds: (1) defined term funds, and (2) defined payout funds.

Both types of funds are dependent on the principal and investment returns. (1) The defined term fund is designed to provide payments over a set period of time. The payments are based on the invested principal and investment returns. Payments are not guaranteed but are designed to keep pace with inflation, and can fluctuate over time depending on investment performance. (2) The defined payout fund is designed to provide a specified payment that is a percentage of the invested capital. This amount is generally set as an annual payout and usually paid from investment returns. However, the investment manager can generally opt to invade the principal if necessary to meet payments amounts. The period of time over which payments are made will depend on the investment performance of the fund.

This type of product usually cannot guarantee that payments will last for a specified period of time or for the participant's life. Thus, these products do not solve the issue of longevity if the participant outlives his/her investment.

The advantage of these options is lower costs because there is no guarantee feature.

Managed retirement income accounts. This is not a product. Rather, it is a service where a professional money manager undertakes to manage the participant's account with the goal of preserving the invested capital. The manager will oversee the monthly payments, and will often recommend that that the participant purchase longevity insurance.

The major advantage of this service is the ability of the participant to retain control of his/her account and can cease or increase payments when so desired. The major disadvantage is that this approach does not offer guaranteed lifetime income for the participant.

III. Summary of Testimony and Council Discussion

1. **DOL review, modify, and/or develop regulatory guidance/ clarification with respect to decumulation of retirement assets, including a defined contribution plan annuity safe harbor, participant education, and investment advice. The guidance/ clarification should be designed to reduce current barriers faced by fiduciaries, plan sponsors, and service providers in their efforts to encourage participants to develop post-retirement income strategies and to consider alternatives in offering income replacement options.**

Modification of the Regulatory Safe Harbor for selecting an Annuity Issuer

The Council received much testimony that underscored the importance to the retirement community that DOL develop guidance designed to provide meaningful assistance to plan sponsors and participants through modifying the safe harbor that governs the selection of an annuity as set forth in Regulation Section 2550.404a-4.

Witnesses consistently requested that DOL establish a more definite safe harbor standard to govern the selection of an annuity issuer which in turn would provide greater certainty for plan fiduciaries. The Council recommends that DOL partner with the National Association of Insurance Commissioners (NAIC) in their effort to examine the appropriateness of one or more of the financial indicators utilized by state insurance departments in their evaluation and ongoing monitoring of domiciled insurance companies, and which could be used as feasible factors in any modified annuity selection safe harbor.

Testimony from many witnesses strongly encouraged DOL to provide guidance on the impact of a fiduciary's duty in evaluating issuers and providers of annuities (or other lifetime income options). In particular, witnesses encouraged and discussed with the Council the importance of modifying the annuity provider selection safe harbor within Regulation Section 2550.404a-4[2] In addition, Mr. Jeffrey Turner, with the Office of Regulations and Interpretations, when addressing the Department's work in the area of lifetime income options, acknowledged that public comments support further consideration or action in three distinct areas, the third of which is a review of the fiduciary standards applicable to the selection of annuity providers in DC plans as it relates to the regulatory safe harbor standards.

In its statement submitted for the record, ACLI stated that many of the concerns that currently impede employer's selection of lifetime income options are a byproduct of perceived fiduciary risk. They further stated that it is difficult to overstate the high level of concern about fiduciary liability with respect to such selection. However, it was acknowledged that a position taken in the final regulations on the selection of annuity providers for distributions from DC plans, at 29 CFR §2550.404a-4, were considered an improvement from Interpretive Bulletin 95-1[3]. ACLI noted that the clarification made by DOL that "the safest available annuity standard" does not apply to DC plans was an extremely positive first step to reducing the magnitude of the fiduciary liability impediment, but that additional guidance is needed. ACLI urged DOL to adopt rules and regulations to make the duties of employers in selecting providers of guaranteed lifetime income products similar to employers' duties in selecting providers of life insurance, disability insurance, or other financial protection products.

ACLI further set forth the following standards that should be incorporated in the modified safe harbor with respect to the fiduciary:

1. The fiduciary should engage in an objective, thorough and analytical search for the purpose of identifying and selecting providers from which to purchase annuities;
2. The fiduciary should appropriately consider and conclude, at the time of selection, that the cost (including fees and commissions) of the

annuity contract is reasonable in relation to the benefits and administrative services to be provided; and
3. If necessary, the fiduciary should consult with an appropriate expert or experts for purposes of compliance with safe harbor provisions.

ACLI suggested that instead of requiring the fiduciary to make a determination about the financial ability of the annuity provider to make all future payments, the safe harbor should require that the fiduciary give consideration to the financial strength and other "quality" aspects of the provider.

In his testimony, Mr. Kevin Hanney, with United Technologies, stated that it is critical for the regulatory agencies to promote a clear and reasonable standard of care for plan sponsors and fiduciaries. He noted that while many will endeavor to develop best-in-class practices as it relates to the design, evaluation, selection, and oversight of income replacement solutions, few will devote their valuable resources to the effort in the absence of a clear and reasonable standard of care. He noted in the absence of such guidance, there exists a very real risk that the plan sponsor and/or fiduciary would be criticized and second-guessed in the event of that unforeseen, unfortunate and unavoidable conditions arise. He noted that the regulatory agencies were well positioned to provide the necessary level of confidence to well-intentioned and procedurally prudent fiduciaries by issuing, and clearly and consistently communicating, a process-focused standard of care for the evaluation, selection and monitoring of income replacement solutions.

In addressing some of the shortcomings of the existing safe harbor, Mr. Ashton, of Drinker Biddle, noted that it does not provide sufficient detail to be a valuable tool for the average plan fiduciary. He noted that it does not clearly address the type of information that should be considered in assessing the ability of an annuity provider to make future payments. In addition, he noted that the safe harbor does not address other retirement income options outside an annuity product. He stated that while the process set forth in the safe harbor regulation would presumably be the same for the selection of other products that it would be helpful if DOL would clarify this.

Mr. Michael Hadley, of Davis and Harmon LLP, is another witness who spoke to this issue and noted that "it is not, and should not be, the law that offering an annuity distribution turns plan fiduciaries into stop-loss guarantors of insurers whose financial condition unexpectedly deteriorates despite the watchful eyes of state insurance commissioners." He noted that it is incumbent upon policymakers –and the attorneys that advise plan fiduciaries –to remove any uncertainty on this point. As noted above, many witnesses focused on review and selection of annuity options, with much attention being focused on meaningful uncertainties many fiduciaries encounter in trying to comply with the annuity selection safe harbor. Witnesses cited this as a significant reason why more employers do not make an annuity option available under the plan. Witnesses stated that the current rule provides less of a safe harbor and more of a statement that the plan fiduciary must predict the financial viability to the annuity issuer not only at the time of purchase, but for the life of the annuity. Some witnesses recommended that plan sponsors be allowed to rely solely on the fact that the annuity issuer is licensed under the state insurance laws and is permitted to conduct business in the state. On the other hand, other witnesses requested that DOL seek insights from the NAIC to identify helpful criteria that could serve as the basis for a safe harbor.

Ms. Julie McPeak testified on behalf of the NAIC and provided an overview of the level of oversight the State insurance regulators engage in with respect to the life insurance and annuity providers domiciled in their particular state and the states in which they are licensed to conduct business. She noted that each life insurance company is subject to minimum valuation requirements, Standard Valuation Law and periodic financial stress tests. She also noted that each life insurance company is required to file a number of financial documents (some annually and others quarterly). In addition, she noted that regulators, at least quarterly, assess certain aspects of the company's business including reserve adequacy, leverage, liquidity and surplus. Commissioner McPeak indicated that she thought some of these documents and processes would be helpful in the evaluation process.

In response to a question from the Council, Ms. McPeak noted that she did not believe it would be sufficient to establish a safe harbor based solely on the fact that a life insurance company and annuity provider is licensed in a state. Instead, she noted that plan sponsors and fiduciaries should take into account the extensive oversight regimen each state has in place to examine and monitor the on-going financial viability of the company. She noted that NAIC's Life Insurance and Annuities (A) committee recently formed a working group to examine and analyze options that would be helpful to employers becoming more confident with the financial viability of annuity providers as included in a safe harbor developed by DOL. Ms. McPeak expressed great interest in working with DOL in this effort.

The Council believes that this partnership could be extremely helpful to DOL in their effort to develop a more workable safe harbor for the selection of annuities and other lifetime income products and would encourage DOL to develop this partnership with NAIC on this issue.

Needed Clarification to Promote Participant Education and Advice on Income Replacement Options

Testimony from multiple witnesses stressed the importance of education for plan participants in understanding the challenges of ensuring financial security during the retirement years when retirement savings is through a DC plan. Witnesses noted the importance of sensitizing plan participants to the challenges of managing the lifetime decumulation of retirement savings, particularly given the significant unknown element -how long the individual and/or spouse will live. The risk of exhausting all retirement assets during the participant's lifetime was stressed in much of the testimony.

Mr. Bruce Ashton testified that more and more workers will face significant risks in retirement, leading to what some have referred to as the post-retirement crisis. Included in these risks is the significant statistical probability that individuals will love longer in retirement than they expect. He further testified that few participants understand how long they can expect to live after retirement, and thus how much money they will need for retirement. He noted that there is a significant probability that retirement funds will need to last for as much as 30 years. This, he said, is a high probability that participants can hardly afford to ignore.

Mr. Jonathan Forman, a professor of Law with University of Oklahoma, in a written submission commented on the risk of participants outliving their retirement savings. He noted that the greatest risk facing current and future retirees with a DC plan is the risk of outliving one's retirement savings. He noted that as life expectancy increases, accumulated retirement savings in individual accounts will need to finance an even greater portion of retirees' ever-longer retirements. He cited the following data: "at present, a 65 year-old woman has an even chance of living past age 86, while a 65 year-old man has an even chance of living past age 84.[4] Also, he noted that today's college students have a 50-50 chance of living to age 100."[5]

Knowing that retirement is likely to be longer than most participants anticipate, and that the money accumulated in the DC plan will be a significant portion, if not substantially all, of the participant's retirement funds, it is imperative that participants begin to view their DC plan retirement funds not as just an accumulation of savings, but a pot of money that must be managed in a way to provide replacement of salary, wages, and other compensation during the participants' retirement years and over their lifetime.

Mr. Kevin Hanney testified that United Technologies Corporation (UTC) recognized the challenge for most plan participants is to grasp a firm understanding of what is necessary for them to construct and implement a savings and investment program during their working years, and subsequently adhere to a disciplined spending program in retirement that when combined is sufficient to sustain a level of income comparable to their salary, wages and other compensation. He noted that UTC decided that participant education should be underpinned with plan features designed to address key employee challenges. To this end, UTC adopted a Lifetime Income Strategy, which is promoted with increased education among their employees.

The Council recognizes that UTC is among the larger employers and therefore does not necessarily set the tone for smaller employers. However, the Council does recognize the critical need for employer involvement if efforts to ensure that workers have a source of lifetime income during retirement years are to succeed. In that regard, the Council sought testimony to determine whether there were specific barriers preventing employers from becoming more involved and providing education to participant on possible investments and distribution options for lifetime income. The Council received testimony on the barriers employers currently face in this effort.

Witnesses identified critical barriers that many employers and service providers face in their effort to adopt greater education tools and distribution options to enable better participant retirement planning.

The Council heard testimony that many employers and service providers rely upon existing DOL guidance applicable to education and guidance to provide important programs to participants. However, witnesses expressed concerns with this approach because this guidance has not been clarified or updated to specifically apply to education and advice on distribution options to ensure lifetime income under a DC plan.

ACLI's statement for the record submitted on June 13, 2012 noted that many employers are hesitant to provided educational information and advice regarding lifetime income options or other arrangements designed to provide an income stream during retirement because of their fear that fiduciary liability would apply to such education and advice. ACLI requested that fiduciaries be afforded protection for the dissemination of information on lifetime distribution options, whether offered under the plan or outside the plan. ACLI reiterated the recommendation that DOL expand Interpretive Bulletin 96-1 to explicitly cover education regarding decumulation strategies such as lifetime income options. ACLI noted that a model notice may prove to be helpful to plan sponsors.

Witnesses noted that plan sponsors are concerned about the ability to utilize many of the same tools permitted under Interpretive Bulletin 96-1, without explicit confirmation from DOL that such reliance is appropriate. Interpretive Bulletin 96-1 was adopted in 1996 to provide the views of DOL concerning participants' directed plans and the circumstances under which providing investment related information would not be considered "investment advice" for ERISA purposes with respect to participants and beneficiaries. The Bulletin identified categories of information and materials under such plans that do not constitute providing investment advice, to invoke the application of "fiduciary" under ERISA section 3(21)(A)(ii) and its corresponding regulation under 29 CFR §2510.3-21(c)(1).

On this issue, Mr. Hanney with UTC stated that the one approach to immediately improve clarity for plan sponsors and plan services providers is to update language in existing guidance to reflect recent product developments and to which products it applies. Mr. Jeffrey Turner, Deputy Director of the Office of Regulations and Interpretations, acknowledged in his testimony that, in the context of DOL's Lifetime Income initiative and in the interest of providing guidance on the education of employees about lifetime income options, the Department is considering an expansion in scope to IB 96-1. Witnesses noted that absent such guidance and clarification, materials and resources intended as participant education could be characterized as investment advice. Similarly, witnesses acknowledged that existing DOL guidance that validates an investment advisory program as being "conflict-free" does not take into account the aspect of plan distributions that can include the selection of lifetime income products including immediate or deferred annuities. Consistent with the recommendations of the witnesses, the Council recommends that DOL provide such confirmations and clarifications.

Many of the witnesses repeatedly requested that the Council recommend that DOL expand the IB 96-1 to provide guidance and clarification on providing information about distribution options that would not be considered investment advice. More specifically, witnesses asked for guidance and clarification on the information and education that can be provided to participants without triggering the application of the fiduciary requirements. Witnesses requested guidance and clarification on information to participants regarding how to structure payout options and extending the scope of the existing prohibited transaction guidance (such as fee leveling guidance, Advisory Opinion 2001-09A, etc...) to include investment advice relating to distributions and distribution options.

In conclusion, multiple witnesses testified that with appropriate revisions and/or clarifications to these issues plan sponsors and fiduciaries would be more willing to provide education and investment advice regarding distribution options and the decumulation process for participants and beneficiaries under a DC plan, including the range of potential economic risks for participants with respect to selecting certain distribution options and the risks of making their retirement savings last over their retirement years. Witnesses requested that DOL's guidance and clarification should make providing education and advice investment with respect to the decumulation phase of the participant's account as available as education and investment advice in the accumulation phase of the account. The witnesses emphasized that the availability of such education and investment advice is crucial to successful lifetime income outcomes for participants.

2. **DOL develop more immediate clarification in the same areas in the form of FAQs or other sub-regulatory guidance while DOL examines the recommendation set forth above.**

The Council recognizes that the process of issuing regulatory guidance and clarification as set forth in the recommendation discussed above is a deliberate process which could require a significant investment of time and DOL's resources. Thus, the Council is aware that the recommendation may not be a prime candidate for expedited action. However, the Council also is convinced of the importance of issuing some level of clarification in the near-term to assist the plan sponsor community to be more pro-active in the area of examining, selecting, and offering lifetime income options to their employees. For this reason, the Council recommends that, in the interim, DOL provide guidance on the issues highlighted and discussed under the above recommendation whether in the form of FAQs or other sub-regulatory guidance. The Council believes that this would go a long way to eliminating the current barriers for plan sponsors and their fear of the application of fiduciary liability in an unclear manner, and that plan participants will benefit from improved education and advice on the consideration and selection of lifetime income products for a secured retirement.

3. **DOL develop educational materials to assist employers and plan sponsors in evaluating and selecting income replacement options. The materials should focus on aspects such as:**

1. **The need to accomplish a shift in the perception of DC plans, to include the importance of planning for the decumulation (retirement distribution) process;**
2. **Commonly applied definitions;**
3. **Features, designs, risks, and trade-offs;**
4. **Roles of a plan sponsor/employer when offering income replacement options, education, and advice;**
5. **Review and evaluation of projection tools used for income replacement stream;**
6. **Lessons from behavioral finance and research about misconceptions related to income strategies, planning horizons, and understanding longevity risks.**

Modifying the Focus of DC Plans to Include Importance of Planning for Income Replacement during Retirement and Possible Options

As stated in an overwhelming majority of the testimony, current participant education efforts are focused on a participant's accumulation of assets and savings. However, the Council, consistent with witness testimony, believes that plan sponsors need to engage participants with educational materials in understanding the importance of, and how to make their retirement savings last over their retirement years. Certain witnesses noted that record keepers and plan sponsors agreed that adequate retirement income will be the biggest issue under DC plans in the years ahead.

Because the original design and goal of DC plans was to provide supplemental retirement income, the focus of retirement savings in this type of plan traditionally has not included a focus on the ability of plan participants to have lifetime replacement income as an integral part of the plan design. However, the changing role of DC plans to becoming the major (and in many cases the only) source of retirement income for many of today's workers has highlighted the need for DC plans to expand their focus to include providing workers with a secured retirement as one of their major goals. This will involve changing the plan's ultimate structure from solely the accumulation of retirement savings to distribution options that include replacing income over the participant's lifetime.

MetLife conducted a study, "*A Study of Retirement Income Culture Among the FORTUNE 1000*," where a key goal was to measure whether large companies are moving beyond their well-ingrained culture of retirement accumulation toward the creation of a culture that places equal emphasis on retirement accumulation and decumulation of retirement income. Specifically, the study sought to assess the extent to which plan sponsors at the FORTUNE 1000 companies are encouraging and supporting ways for workers to prepare for their income needs in retirement.

In the study, MetLife observed that a substantial majority of plan sponsors appear to recognize the importance of cultivating a retirement philosophy that not only focuses on providing cost-effective retirement benefits that help them remain competitive, but also inculcates the importance of their employees creating retirement income to their futures. However, the study found that despite recognizing the importance of retirement income, plan sponsors remain more focused on retirement savings than on retirement income as a key objective of their programs. In the study, while 93% say that retirement savings is extremely important as a focus of their retirement plans, only 65% say retirement income has a comparable level of importance or their retirement program.

The study found that where plan sponsors have retirement income as a key focus of their philosophy regarding their retirement plan, they are much more likely than other plan sponsors to recognize the ability to generate retirement income as a very important measure of success.

In supporting a need for such a modification, Mr. Srinivas D. Reddy, with Prudential Financial, noted that pursuant to "*Prudential Retirement Plan Participant Survey, 2012*" only one in five participants is "extremely or very" confident that their money will last through retirement. Prudential noted that in two studies they conducted there were three outcome-oriented benefits of shifting the focus to retirement income. The study noted that participants save more, maintain diverse portfolios, and stay the course even in period of high volatility. From the survey Prudential also noted that the data showed that when an in-plan guaranteed retirement income option is offered that participants contributed more.

This data clearly supports the Council's recommendation that there is a need for plan sponsors and 401(k) providers to provide more participant education that is focused on lifetime income options in DC plans.

Commonly Applied Definitions for Income Replacement Products

As noted throughout this report, there are several alternatives available to plan sponsors and participants in the area of income replacement, including:[6]

- **Fixed Life Annuity**
  This product is based on the payment of level income (which may also include a fixed annual increase, or cost of living adjustment (COLA)) paid for life. Either single life or joint life options are typically available. The product may include an initial minimum guarantee period so that in the event of death prior to the end of the guarantee period, income continues to be paid to the beneficiary until the end of the guarantee period.
- **Variable Life Annuity**
  Under this product, income is paid for life. The amount of income varies each year based on the performance of the underlying funds. Consumers can choose allocations among various underlying funds. Under this product, either single life or joint life options are typically available. The product may include an initial minimum guarantee period so that in the event of death prior to the end of the guarantee period, income continues to be paid to the beneficiary until the end of the guarantee period.
- **Fixed Period Annuity**
  The product has level income amounts (which may also include a COLA) that are paid for a fixed period.
- **Systematic Withdrawals**
  This option includes withdrawals taken from a deferred annuity or a retirement fund on a systematic basis. It can be set up to accommodate almost any pattern of income. Once the fund is fully liquidated, income payments cease.
- **Interest Only Withdrawals**
  This is a form of systematic withdrawals where the earnings on a retirement fund are paid out as income on a periodic basis.
- **Longevity Insurance**
  This option is a lifetime annuity with benefits that start at a specified future date or advanced age (i.e. 85). When used in combination with a systematic withdrawal program from a retirement asset, the combination provides income and the flexibility of an emergency fund

for several years in retirement that is followed by fixed lifetime income.

- **Guaranteed Lifetime Withdrawal Benefit (GLWB)**
  This is typically in the form of a rider to a variable annuity. It provides a guaranteed withdrawal amount (typically around 5% for a 65 year old) from a deferred annuity account such that once the account is fully liquidated, the guaranteed withdrawal amount continues to be received as long as the consumer lives.
- **Guaranteed Minimum Income Benefit (GMIB)**
  This is typically in the form of a rider to a variable annuity. It provides a guaranteed minimum lifetime income amount per $1,000 of accumulated value, where the accumulated value is guaranteed to increase regardless of the performance of underlying funds.
- **Target Income or Managed Payout Funds**
  This is in the form of mutual funds that seek to provide an annual income that is based on a fixed period (where the income varies) or a fixed percentage of original investment (where how long the income will last varies).
- **Lump Sum**
  This is in the form of a one-time, single payout of the entire proceeds of a retirement savings account. Once the lump sum payment is made, the recipient can use the funds for any purpose, but there is no further amount payable from the account.

Available Income Replacement Alternative -Features, Designs, Risks, Tradeoffs

The Council heard testimony from many witnesses weighing in on this topic with one theme emerging as a consistent message -DOL should develop educational materials to help plan sponsors effectively evaluate and select income replacement options. A major part of effectively evaluating and selecting the income options is understanding the key features, designs, risks, and tradeoffs of the options being considered.

Witnesses provided input on the broad availability of retirement products. In general, the options can be separated into two categories: (1) withdrawal income options (with no lifetime guarantees) and (2) lifetime income with payment guarantees. A major concern with the withdrawal income options is that participants could outlive the payment period designed under the option, whereas, the dominant concern with lifetime income is that the participant has to give up some or all of the control over, and generally access to the assets in the case of an emergency.

Witnesses emphasized that one particular retirement distribution option, an annuity (in its various forms, including: immediate annuities, longevity annuities, joint and survivor annuities, and annuities with various guarantees), though not a solution for every participant's situation, is one of the few options that guarantees income for life.

Mr. Srinvas D. Reddy noted that are a number of options available to DC plan participants with regards to the creation of retirement income, which can be grouped into in-plan versus out-of-plan solutions and best efforts versus guaranteed solutions. He noted in the attempt to address the primary retirement income risk of longevity that there is a tradeoff between the amount of income generated and the level of flexibility and control the participant retains.

Mr. Reddy testified that the primary out-of-plan solution offered through the workplace consist of various immediate annuities, of which fixed immediate payout annuities are predominant. In-plan options, on the other hand, have expanded through innovation over the past several years. He noted that best efforts products include managed payout mutual funds and managed accounts with systematic withdrawal programs. Guaranteed products encompass payout annuities, longevity insurance and hybrid innovations such as guaranteed lifetime (minimum) withdrawal benefit (GLWB/GMWB).

Managed payout funds are essentially mutual fund investments that create ongoing retirement income as the fund's investment objective. The payout rate will determine whether the retirement income is paid with or without preservation of the principal investment. Mr. Srinvas noted that these products may be attractive due to the simplicity of the design or the familiarity of the structure to participants who are familiar with mutual funds. Also, he noted that a significant challenge is to ensure that the plan participant understands that these solutions are not guaranteed and that resulting investment performance and retirement income risk are retained by the participant.

Additional testimony highlighted the lower relative cost of annuitization as a result of the pooling of mortality risks across annuitants, along with the tradeoffs of the corresponding possibility that the participant might die prematurely and forfeit a substantial portion of the annuity purchase. This pooling of risks, witnesses noted, could result in a significant discount on cost up to a 30 percent reduction. Witnesses noted the importance of showing plan sponsors, fiduciaries, and participants that an annuity provides insurance against exhausting an individual's retirement savings. They also noted a potential for balancing the opposing considerations by including additional guarantees in the annuity for an additional cost.

Role of Employer/Plan Sponsor – Educating Plan Participants, Providing Advice

The Council believes that plan sponsors should adapt their education efforts to engage participants in a dialog to develop a better understanding of how to make their retirement savings last a lifetime. This will be especially important as the wave of the baby-boom generation enters into their retirement years. Education around income replacement will be of paramount importance and will play a pivotal role in increasing the probability of making their assets last throughout their lifetime. The Council heard from many witnesses and was informed that education will not be easy, due to the complex nature of the various lifetime income products and options that are available in the marketplace.

Moreover, witnesses strongly recommended that the educational information allowed explicitly permit the provision of information to employees regarding retirement risks, the definition of a longevity market, inflation, retirement, etc. Also, it was recommended that the educational guidance be permitted to include retirement income models, retirement calculators and annuity illustrations, while avoiding the risk of it being characterized as providing "investment advice" within the meaning of the existing regulations and IB 96-1. The educational information, as proposed, should also include the different types of products offered, their features and risks, and the costs of the income replacement products that may be offered.

The various options and the corresponding complexity can be intimidating to both a plan sponsor as well as plan participants. For this reason, the Council recommends that DOL champion the idea of creating a guide which explains the basic definitions that are used when examining and evaluating lifetime income products. In addition, the guide should include a discussion on the different types of products, features, designs, risks, tradeoffs, and promote the development and adoption of income replacement options.

The Council heard testimony from Ms. Cynthia Mallet of MetLife, who discussed her company's recently released study entitled "*Perspectives of Plan Sponsors and Recordkeepers for Qualified Plans*." The study explored the dynamics of the plan sponsor and record keeper relationship and the efforts they are making to provide participants with the necessary education, tools, awareness and solutions as well as identify the perceived obstacles to providing retirement income options under DC plans.

Many witnesses agreed that employers would be more inclined to consider offering lifetime income products if DOL would provide more guidance on their roles and responsibilities when offering income replacement options, education, and advice. ACLI, in its submitted testimony, stated that "DOL should clarify that plan assets may be used to educate participants about lifetime income options including those typically available outside of the plan. Without this clarification, plan sponsors, who are in the best position to ensure that participants receive this information, may hesitate to do so and plan service providers may be reluctant to include education on lifetime income as part of their service models."

Kevin Hanney stated, with respect to clear and reasonable guidance on plan sponsor education, "we respectfully submit that draft guidance issued by relevant regulatory agencies and meaningful comment periods will be crucial to successfully addressing the many issues plan sponsors face." This information supports the Council's recommendation that plan sponsors need some guidance and clarity to help them move more fully into the income replacement options area.

Review and Evaluation of Income Replacement Projection Tools

Witnesses also discussed the value of online income tools as an education reference. There appears to be difficulty among participants in understanding their account balances as reflected in terms of a stream of income due, in large part, to the degree of complexity involved in using these income projection tools. For example, assumption rates and the rate of return calculated in the results given to participants are not easily defined and depend largely on the tool used. The Council encourages DOL to develop additional educational materials that would advise participants of the tools available, and guide participants on how to use these tools to their advantage.

The Council was advised that these tools should include a variety of mortality assumptions that a participant can utilize in order to project a broad range of retirement outcomes when evaluating possible options. To that end, the Council encourages DOL to review its online retirement calculator that is already available via its online publication, *Taking the Mystery out of Retirement Planning*, and develop a calculator that provides an estimate of the monthly payment of a lifetime benefit under a particular amount of retirement savings. The use of such a calculator could serve as a general guideline for participants to understand the amount an individual would receive under a specific scenario and could prompt participants to adjust personal savings as needed.

Testimony supported showing participants the projected income stream under their account as well as the accumulated account balances on their benefit statements.

Although using the participant account statement to illustrate the income stream that can be produced by an account balance was supported, in general, by the witnesses, there was considerable disagreement over what details should be provided on the statements. For example, it was debated whether to encourage or mandate illustrations of the income stream and whether the current account balance of the participant was appropriate to provide the projection. Some witnesses advised that plan sponsors did not want a mandate to provide this information to their participants.

Because the Council is aware that DOL is already working on this issue as part of pension benefit statement guidance with the Treasury Department, the Council decided not to make any recommendation with respect to this issue. However, the Council notes that this it is an important issue that, if implemented correctly, can go a long way to help in the overall educational process.

Understanding Longevity Risks, Planning Horizons etc.

A significant amount of witness testimony was received expressing the need for educational materials and outreach to assist participants in understanding the complexities of income replacement options. It was expressed that a lack of participant focus on the importance of lifetime income leads to a lack of diversity in investment, low deferral rates and loss aversion. Witnesses recommended that if participants were expected to save a sufficient amount to produce lifetime replacement income then the participants' focus should be on the importance of planning retirement goals. Witnesses testified that participants need to be given basic financial education so that they can better understand how much retirement savings they will need to adequately produce replacement income throughout retirement.

Many witnesses noted that participants lack understanding of the various lifetime income options available to them. Some stated that while participants like the aspect of receiving a steady stream of income for life, with no risk of running out of money, they are concerned about the cost of the products and the aspect of losing control over the funds they must release .

Richard Bailey with VALIC stated, with respect to employers and plan sponsors addressing these issues, that "these types of analyses can be quite complex depending on the circumstances and financial assets of the participant. While the employer may not be obligated to provide more sophisticated planning which could include retirement savings or financial assets outside of the plan, the ability to offer that level of planning may aid the employer in attracting and retaining employees."

Mr. Hanney testified that "most individuals do not possess the knowledge, resources and/or incentives that are necessary to construct and implement a savings and investment program during their working years…" He further stated that if left to this independently, many individuals underestimate their retirement needs and the level of savings necessary to fund those needs. He noted that at UT they were not mistaken about the level of education an employee needs, and how essential such education was to successful outcomes.

Richard Pretty, with TIAA-CREF, stated that his company's experience has shown that many participants do not understand how much income they will need in retirement, how much they need to save prior to retirement, and fail to properly convert their DC plan retirement savings into adequate income once they reach retirement. He also noted that their research shows that keeping education simple and leveraging "inertia" can help produce better outcomes.

Additionally, some witnesses noted that two common questions from individuals considering lifetime income products are how much to annuitize and the security/safety of insurance companies. Education efforts could be focused on consideration of the participant's total financial picture in determining how much to annuitize. While it is clear that employers will not have access to much of this information, the employer could make the employees aware of the importance to taking a total financial approach to these issues. The issues surrounding the security and safety of providers of lifetime income products is discussed more fully under the recommendation set forth in number one.

DOL's participant education and outreach should include information that is geared towards a typical age period of a participant. The Council recommends that DOL outreach begins with participants as early as possible so that they can more accurately evaluate their retirement income goals. Acknowledging that DOL's current materials reference the need for a participant's retirement portfolio to be diverse, the material should be enhanced to discuss the need to understand portfolio risk and what impact market volatility has on that risk. The guidance should include an overall evaluation of a participant's lifetime income needs, factoring lifestyle choices and other household income, including spousal retirement income, survivorship benefits, etc.

4. **DOL develop educational materials to assist individuals in understanding and choosing income replacement options to best suit their retirement needs, including:**
   a) **The importance of understanding the life-cycle approach to planning;**
   b) **Key features, designs, risks, and trade-offs;**
   c) **The importance of understanding the tools and assumptions used to project income stream;**
   d) **The need to evaluate all household sources of retirement income, including survivor benefits and Social Security;**
   e) **The impact of inflation and inflation assumptions;**
   f) **Understanding the impact of longevity and longevity risk, the need for a long planning horizon and potential benefits from mortality risk pooling;**
   g) **The timing of decisions and alternatives.**

a) The Importance of Understanding the Life-Cycle Approach to Planning

The Council concluded that DOL should develop life-cycle planning materials to help individuals understand the importance of planning at each stage of their working life. Witnesses testified, and the Council believes, that this type of planning will assist individuals to set retirement goals and generate sufficient lifetime income to cover retirement expenses.

Professor Olivia Mitchell and other witnesses documented the formidable challenge of individuals with DC plans who need to ensure their own retirement security. Many individuals underestimate their retirement needs and the level of savings necessary to fund them. Mr. Reddy with Prudential noted in his testimony that a disproportionate focus on current financial demands, coupled with a lack of education regarding financial needs during retirement, leaves many participants unaware of their true retirement income needs.

As more individuals rely on building savings in defined contribution plans, it becomes even more important to use this planning approach to develop better savings, avoid mistakes and implement a financial strategy that shifts as the individual ages. The Council heard testimony from other witnesses that suggested the importance of continuing to promote savings during the accumulation phase; to provide individuals with benchmarks to help them stay on track to reach the amount they will need to retire; and to know how that savings will translate into monthly payments that will cover their expenses during retirement.

As noted in testimony received, life-cycle planning helps individuals by identifying broad guidelines to help keep them on track to meet their financial goals. The life-cycle approach promotes financial priorities for each stage of life as follows:

- During the early stage of accumulation, **age 25-35**, individuals should begin to contribute to a 401(k) or IRA account, build up an emergency fund and start to save for a down payment for a home. An appropriate benchmark would be to advise individuals that building up their savings contributions to 10-15 percent of salary is the retirement savings goal for their working lives.
- The next stage, **age 35-50**, is the time to be saving as much as possible for retirement, taking advantage of the power of compounding, saving for children's college and achieving a high rate of return on investments.
- Generally, those **age 50-60,** are in their peak earning years. They need to assess where they are in relation to their retirement goals, take full advantage of the catch-up provisions, and begin to evaluate their employer-sponsored plan distribution options. For those **age 60 and older,** both pre-retiree and retirees need to understand their appropriate portfolio risk and make sure that they are protecting themselves against sudden market volatility. e.g., a sudden loss that they will not have the time to make up for in the few years before retirement.

The Council recommends that DOL's participant education and outreach should include information that highlights the retirement saving goals during a typical age period of a participant. The Council further recommends that DOL outreach begins with participants as early as possible so that they can more accurately evaluate their retirement income goals.

b) The Key Features, Designs, Risks, and Trade-Offs

The Council recommends that DOL provide Tip Sheets on the many different types of lifetime income options that are available and the various risks and tradeoffs of each choice.

The Council received testimony from witnesses that addressed the issue of a lack of understanding of the various lifetime income options, and the differences among the available options. Many witnesses noted that while there is no simple solution to address every individual's concerns about the best lifetime income replacement option for their particular situation, that these decisions are best made with the inclusion of an overall evaluation of a participant's lifetime income needs, factoring lifestyle choices and other household income, including spousal retirement income, survivorship benefits, etc.

Other witnesses noted that the features that appeal most to individuals are those that provide guaranteed income for the rest of one's life with the elimination of the risk of running out of money. However, it was noted that there is some tension for most individuals who either do not want to pay for the elimination of that risk because of the cost or there linquishment of control, or they do not fully understand the benefits vs. the risks of the product they are purchasing. The features that individuals view as disadvantages are those where the decision is irrevocable, the product is inflexible and the funds are inaccessible.

Other factors that individuals must consider include the fees, commissions, and other charges associated with each product, as well as the financial health of the insurance provider of the guaranteed income product. The table below[7] highlights some of the features, designs, risks and tradeoffs of some of the broader categories of income replacement strategies and options:

c) The Importance of Understanding the Tools and Assumptions Used to Project Income Stream

The Council recommends that DOL develop education materials that would help individuals gain access to, and understand the application of, tools that convert a savings amount/account balance into a lifetime income stream.

Most witnesses stated that DC plans leave individuals with the difficult task of figuring out how to understand their retirement savings goal. Most witnesses agreed that individuals are unprepared for this task and need professional help, including calculations to translate account balances into a steady stream of income. Some of the witnesses expressed concern that even with the availability of some projection tools that many individuals do not have the specialized expertise or access to the skills that would enable them to successfully apply these tools.

Features	Income Annuity	Other Products with Guarantees	Withdrawals
Guaranteed income for life	Yes	Yes, but at a lower level than in income annuity	No
Mortality leveraging	Yes	Some	No
Liquidity/access to funds	Not in most products	Yes, within limits	Yes
Remaining account value goes to heirs on death	No	Yes, after fees for guarantees	Yes
Owner can control funds in the account while income is being paid out	No	Yes, within limits	Yes

Source: Society of Actuaries 2012 Decision Brief: Designing a Monthly Paycheck for Retirement.

It was noted that while there are many retirement planning tools available to help retirees calculate their retirement savings as projected into an income stream, there is a degree of sophistication needed to successfully use these tools and receive an accurate projection. For example, an individual would need to understand the assumptions used with respect to, among other things, the expected rate of return for the underlying investments and the rate of inflation.

The Council acknowledges that DOL's online tool and publication, *Taking the Mystery Out of Retirement Planning,* helps those individuals who are close to retirement (age 50 and older) estimate their retirement savings and evaluate if they are on track for their retirement goals. The Council encourages DOL to modify this online tool to provide options to a broader range of users and allow them to apply the tool to their retirement savings at an earlier age, and enable them to assess the conversion of all or part their employer-based retirement savings into a lifetime or immediate annuity providing for estimated monthly payments under the chosen option. The Council believes that this expanded application will result in helping individuals evaluate their retirement goals more effectively.

d) The Need to Evaluate All Household Sources of Retirement Income, Including Survivor Benefits and Social Security

Although retirement planning can be challenging for individuals it is important for head of households to put a retirement strategy in place that includes the evaluation of all sources of retirement income. The strategy should include knowledge of which sources of income are in the form of guaranteed lifetime payments, if there is inflation protection on any of the retirement income options, and if there are funds available for emergencies or some other form of flexibility. This "total picture" approach to retirement will require the individual to seek some level of professional help at some point in time, but the Council believes that improved education in the employer-based system could significantly prepare individuals to be better able to successfully approach the "total picture" planning stage.

A major source of retirement income is likely to be from the individual's employer-based plan . If the individual has retirement benefits under a DB plan he/she is more likely to have some form of lifetime income option. If, however, the individual has retirement benefits under a DC plan, the issues discussed in this report will apply, and the individual must take the initiative to seek such lifetime income options. These options may be accessed either through the employer-based plan or outside the plan through, more typically an IRA. Other sources of retirement income include survivor benefits and Social Security benefits. In most cases these benefits are paid in the form of lifetime income options but generally are not protected for inflation. Some witnesses noted that Social Security will be the dominant source of income for many individuals, and for those who have benefits under a DB or DC plan that these sources of income will play a critical role in providing retirement security.

Decisions about *when* to commence benefits, including Social Security benefits, can themselves have a significant impact on the retirement income adequacy for an individual or a couple. For example, for some individuals or couples, delaying the start of Social Security benefits (which might require substitution of other retirement income sources, or even continued work, during the period of the delay) can provide significant increases in retirement income overall. For others, claiming sooner may better facilitate needed retirement income.

Some witnesses stated that it is also important to note if an individual has a Social Security benefit, a DB plan benefit, access to employer-provided retiree health insurance, and a fully paid home mortgage, there may be a reduced need for additional lifetime income guarantee, as in such a case most of the individual's living expenses would be covered.

e) The Impact of Inflation and Inflation Assumptions

The Council recommends that DOL provide inflation charts with examples on how the inflation factor apply to certain products in order to help individuals understand the importance of planning for the effect of inflation during the retirement years.

Stephen Sexauer highlighted the five dominant risks which affect individuals: the risk of not saving enough; longevity risk or outliving savings; investment risk including inflation risk; counterparty risk; and liquidity risk. He noted that inflation becomes a major issue as people spend more time in retirement. Olivia Mitchell noted that it is also a primary risk that many individuals ignore. She stated that it is important for individuals to be made aware of how the inflation risk will substantially reduce their purchasing power and threaten their long-term financial security in retirement. Thus, it is important for individuals to have inflation protected income options to enable the individuals to maintain their standard of living in retirement.

Some witnesses spoke to the importance for individuals to know the impact of medical care and medical costs in retirement, and pointed out that medical care has a higher inflation rate than the annual U.S. inflation rate. The witnesses also noted that many individuals underestimate the high costs associated with medical care in their retirement years.

f) Understanding of Longevity and Longevity Risk and the Need for a Long Planning Horizon. Potential Benefits from Mortality Risk Pooling

The Council recommends that DOL develop education materials that focus specifically on, and are designed to encourage individuals to incorporate, the long-term aspect of retirement planning. The materials should provide an explanation of the impact of longevity risk on lifetime retirement security. Longevity risk in this context is defined as the risk that participants will outlive their assets and run out of money during retirement. Also, the materials should address the potential benefit of risk pooling.

Most witnesses agreed that many individuals do not know how to manage the risks of longevity, and that there are gaps in the knowledge individuals have that prevent them from effectively dealing with these risks. Kevin Hanney's testimony suggests that the Lifetime Income program established by United Technologies provides evidence that offering a lifetime option to participants that is accessible throughout the accumulation phase is an important way to increase annuitization by plan participants. This behavior was also confirmed by testimony from Richard Pretty with TIAA-CREF.

Mr. Sexauer reminded the Council that there is no risk-free solution to retirement income and while we can point out the risks and the decisions involved in managing the risks in order to get retirees to where they need to be, there is a need for longevity pooling which provides large gains and up to 30% fewer assets needed to fund a given level of retirement income. During the discussion sessions, the Council was made aware that participants do not focus on the mortality pooling issue but discovered that it is an opportunity to achieve a superior return on the investment if they outlive others in the pooled lives. He noted, along with Olivia Mitchell and Kelli Hueler, that participants generally focus more on losing control of their money and dying before the projected age. Ms. Mitchell noted that pooling was a good investment return and that the risks were worthy of insuring. She noted that insuring longevity risk was as important as purchasing automobile or home insurance, yet people more readily accept purchasing these other forms of insurance.

As part of the education effort, Mr. Sexauer also suggested establishing a decumulation benchmark to minimize the four major risks involved in decumulation: longevity, investment (including inflation), counter-party and liquidity risks. Two additional risks were added to the Council's discussion: the sequence of returns risk and the cognitive risk.

The sequence of return is the risk an individual may encounter if he/she uses the drawdown decumulation method. The sequence of the returns the individual would receive over the drawdown period has a significant impact on how long the asset will last. For example, the individual may be withdrawing amounts equal to 5 percent a year, but if there is a negative performance in the asset early in the drawdown phase it will have a significant impact on how long that asset will last versus if the negative returns occur later during the drawdown period.

Also, there is cognitive risk. Cognitive risk affects the consumer or retiree if individuals are making decisions throughout retirement with respect to how they are drawing down their income. At an older-age, illnesses may come into play and the cognitive risk issue becomes very important and difficult to manage. Addressing this risk in the selected option is another positive aspect of a guaranteed income product –eliminating the need to make decisions on how to structure the drawdown features during a period when the individual's cognitive ability is compromised.

g) The timing of decisions and alternatives

The Council recommends that DOL provide education on the key decisions people will face in evaluating their retirement needs including when to initiate retirement payments, what forms of payments to select, and how the get the most from their retirement dollars.

The Council is aware of the overwhelming complexity of evaluating and making effective retirement decisions and that these decisions are unique to each individual. In addition, the Council is aware that analysis and these decisions are beyond the average individual's ability to assess all the relevant risks. Several witnesses mentioned this almost universal problem and acknowledged that the wrong decisions will lead to bad retirement outcomes.

Decisions about when to commence Social Security benefits was highlighted by witnesses (including Olivia Mitchell and Kevin Hanney) as having a potentially significant impact on the retirement income adequacy for an individual or a couple. For some individuals or couples, delaying the start of these benefits (which might require substitution of other retirement income sources, or even continued work, during the period of the delay) can provide significant increases in overall retirement income but for others, claiming these benefits sooner may be the best option to facilitate needed retirement income.

Mr. Sexauer's testimony included a suggestion for a public benchmark to help individuals make an informed choice, measure risks and compare and react to events to help them make better future choices

Other Important Issues

The Council notes the issues highlighted below as issues that received a great deal of attention and discussion during the deliberation of the income replacement topic. The Council could not reach a consensus on whether to include these issues as recommendations, in large part, because resolution of these issues will require an involved process either by DOL, the retirement community, and/or a future Council. However, the Council believes it was necessary to mention the following issues as being fully discussed.

A. Auto Enrollment or Other Default Features for Income Replacement Option Which Could Include a Safe Harbor

The Council heard testimony suggesting the DOL look into the feasibility of adding an auto-enrollment or other default type features for income replacement options which could include a safe harbor option.

Mr. Kevin Hanney, from United Technologies Corporation, suggested the concept of a Qualified Retirement Income Alternative ("QRIA"), which would be designed to achieve the goal of developing and adopting effective income replacement solutions. In addition, the issue of offering a default annuity was also addressed in a June 2011 Government Accountability Office (GAO) report titled "*Retirement Income -Ensuring Income throughout Retirement Requires Difficult Choices.*" The report states that with the declining availability of DB plans and the lifetime retirement income they frequently provide, a default annuity offered within DC plans could help to promote lifetime retirement income for more participants. However, the report did acknowledge there are a few disadvantages with default annuities, such as irreversibility of the election of the option, and/or financial penalties.

Recognizing the success of the current auto enrollment and escalation approaches being adopted and utilized by plan sponsors, the Council believes that the concept of auto enrollment features for income replacement options under DC plans merits further study.

B. Barriers to Plan Sponsor Acting as a Facilitator of Income Replacement Options Outside an Employer-Sponsored Plan

The Council heard testimony regarding the possibility of plan sponsors acting as a facilitator of income replacement options that are offered outside the scope of an employer-sponsored plan. Many of the witnesses testified that the option of participants purchasing an annuity outside an employer-sponsored plan can be very expensive because it is often purchased on an individual basis.

The Council believes that plan sponsors and participants could benefit from further exploration of this concept that would examine ways an employer could assist participant gain access to these options, as well as influence the purchase structure of the benefit for participants.

C. Income Illustration of Account Balances Translated As a Lifetime Stream of Income

Many witnesses testified that it would be very helpful to participants if their account balance is illustrated as a potential income stream on their benefit statements. The witnesses shared their thoughts during the discussion period that this would be more likely to get participants thinking about how their account balance could provide them with replacement income during retirement.

The Council noted that this is an issue that DOL is currently working on. Therefore, the Council notes that the issue was discussed by witnesses and Council members but the Council refrains from making any further recommendations or suggestions.

Conclusion

After receiving testimony and extensive deliberations, the Council concluded that the efforts necessary to sustain lifetime income for a participant in a retirement plan will take a cooperative effort between the plan sponsor and the participant. As part of the effort, participants should be made to recognize the risks inherent in DC plans that did not necessarily exist in more traditional DB plans, specifically, that participants may spend down their assets before their death.

Therefore, guidance by way of educational information offered by a plan sponsor is necessary but the effect on fiduciary responsibility for plan sponsors providing this information appears to be hindering this progress. Moreover, offering lifetime income options may resolve the underlying issue regarding the spend-down of assets. However, a lack of concrete guidance on whether exemptions from fiduciary liability exist for the plan sponsor is preventing many sponsors from offering these options to their employees.

It is the view of the Council that the prospect of a participant not maintaining a lifetime income stream from his or her retirement plan is a serious issue. It is because of this risk that the Council has made the recommendations contained in this report.

Appendix A. Witness Summaries

Jeffrey Turner
Deputy Director, Office of Regulations and Interpretations
Employee Benefits Security Administration, Department of Labor

Jeffrey Turner, Deputy Director of the Office of Regulations and Interpretations, testified for the Employee Benefits Security Administration of the Department of Labor. Mr. Turner thanked the Advisory Council for addressing the issue of income replacement in a DC system and stated that these issues are important to the Department.

Mr. Turner noted that while the decision about including a retirement income product is a settlor, non-fiduciary act, the implementation of the decision is a fiduciary function requiring exercise of fiduciary responsibility. Citing FAB 2007-01, he noted that a fiduciary selecting an investment services provider must engage in a process to review quality of service and fees, as well as potential conflicts of interest. In the context of traditional annuities, he noted the importance of the long-term viability of the provider while acknowledging this may be less important where the choice of an annuity can be changed by the participant. He noted the concerns regarding DOL's regulatory safe harbor on annuity selection, and commented on the low take-up rate of annuities when offered to participants.

Mr. Turner discussed DOL's lifetime income initiative under which they are considering ways to facilitate the provision of lifetime income options in both DC plans and individual retirement accounts (IRAs). He noted the effort included a joint Request for Information that was issued with the Treasury Department. He stated they received more than 700 written comments, conducted two days of public hearings, and received testimony from 45 witnesses. The response suggested action in three different areas:

- Using the participant account statement to illustrate an income stream that could be produced from a given account balance. He noted that there was widespread support for this concept but considerable disagreement over the details to be included. He stated that DOL is working on this issue and hoped that guidance would be issued soon.
- Clarifying the ability of employers to educate their employees about lifetime income options, including possibly amending IB 96-1 (which clarifies that providing education is not considered providing investment advice) to cover education about the spenddown phase Education about the spend-down phase, according to commenters, could include information on the benefits and risks of annuities, longevity risk, interactive tools, and the benefits and risks of in-plan vs. out-of-plan solutions.
- Reviewing the annuity provider selection safe harbor for defined contribution plans.

DOL is looking into each of these areas but intends to start with educational initiatives: lifetime income illustrations in pension benefit statements and IB 96-1.

Dr. Olivia S. Mitchell

Professor of Insurance, Risk Management, Business Economics & Policy

The Wharton School; Director, Pension Research Council and Boettner Center for Pensions & Retirement Security

In written and oral testimony, Dr. Mitchell explained the issues of longevity risk; distinguished annuities from other forms of investments; identified some of the challenges plan sponsors face; and made a number of recommendations concerning how lifetime income options are presented.

Longevity Risk: Dr. Mitchell confirmed that annuities offer longevity risk protection, so people don't outlive their assets. She noted that approximately half of individuals outlive their life expectancy but that mortality varies depending on occupation, race, gender, and other factors. Thereby, making annuitization more, or less, attractive for certain identifiable groups. That some individuals fail to annuitize because they underestimate the chances they will live a long time. She noted that an annuity is not only an investment product, but also insurance of longevity risk, peace of mind, and income protection. She stated that this form of insurance was as important as home owners or automobile insurance, yet individuals were more willing to insure these risks than the risk of outliving their retirement assets.

Choice of Payout Alternatives: Dr. Mitchell highlighted the lack of behavioral economic studies that confirm the impact of a lifetime income payout "default." She noted that while an annuity/lifetime income product provides protection against outliving assets, phased distribution alternatives offer flexibility with each option providing benefits and restrictions. Dr. Mitchell noted that few DC plans offer annuities, and many defined benefit pensions offer lump sums.

Recommendations: Dr. Mitchell recommended that (1) more plan sponsors offer lifetime income options once new safe harbors/guidelines are issued; (2) communicating with regards to lifetime income issues should include information on both immediate and deferred payouts. She noted that educational materials should express financial information in dollar terms rather than percentages because research suggests that participants better understand dollar terms over percentages.

She noted that individual benefit statement or projection of income stream could be wildly off target due to a lack of information, and should include as much specific information as possible. She stated that because the need for lifetime income is increasing as Baby Boomers retire, there need to be changes to enhance the appeal of annuities which can be accomplished, perhaps through increased financial literacy, greater transparency, and other educational means.

With respect to receiving Social Security benefits, Dr. Mitchell noted that Social Security is the best annuitized lifetime income option available to participants. She noted that one of the greatest investment return is to delay the receipt of Social Security benefits until the participant reaches age 70. She noted that a Social Security study showed how claiming rates are affected by how the benefits are presented; Social Security claiming rates accelerated by two years where a "break-even" approach was used.

Bruce Ashton
Partner
Drinker Biddle & Reath

Mr. Ashton testified with regards to why he believed post-retirement income replacement or income protection options were necessary and the policy and legal issues that should be considered with respect to such options. He noted the importance of encouraging the development and use of these options in light of the increased potential for people to outlive their retirement savings. He also noted that cognitive impairment was a key issue. In addition, he stated that most employees have misconceptions regarding how long a single lump sum of money will last, an outgrowth, he sees, from the DC plan retirement system.

Mr. Ashton noted three areas on which policy makers, employees and employers should focus to address the lack of adequate retirement income throughout an employee's lifetime.

- *Participant Education*: Employees need to be given basic financial education to help them better understand how much retirement savings they will need to sustain them throughout their retirement. One way to accomplish this, he noted, would be to include projections on benefit statements which he believes are generally a good communication vehicle. In addition, he also noted that regulatory safe harbors would help encourage education efforts.

- *Employer Education*: Employers need to better understand that their employees will not have enough savings at retirement to last until their deaths. Furthermore, he noted, employers do not appear to be aware of, or interested in, the income protection and replacement options currently available in the marketplace.
- *Regulatory Environment*: The regulatory environment should promote flexibility. Mandates in his area would likely not be effective due to the vast array of products, providers, plans, and employers involved. He stated that he tends to favor "in-plan" options because their use could be promoted under the plan. He further stated that in order to encourage implementation by employers clarity is necessary regarding (i) the fiduciary issues surrounding adopting or implementing lifetime income solutions and (ii) portability of products including the ability to move the benefit from one plan to another, and to activate the benefit at retirement.

Mr. Ashton noted that a key part of the legal analysis underlying income protection solutions is determining whether the products should be analyzed as a distribution option or an investment option. He noted that Section 404(c)'s fiduciary protections for participant-directed investment decisions and for qualified default investment alternatives could be useful. In addition, he stated that he did not believe a formulaic safe harbor would work in the area of selecting and implementing income protection solutions because of the variety of products and services. Rather, he recommended "soft guidance" regarding what DOL believes would be appropriate factors in considering products, and providers and making other decisions would be very helpful and encourage adoption of this approach.

Michael Hadley
Partner
Davis & Harman

Mr. Hadley primarily focused on the legal uncertainties that exist in the area of adopting both "in-plan" and "out-of-plan" income protection options. He noted that while legal uncertainty is not the only reason a lot of employers have not implemented the options, removal of existing legal uncertainty is immediately actionable by policy makers and could yield positive results.

Mr. Hadley discussed several topics that can be addressed by the Department of Labor including the following:

- Clarification of the "plan asset" status of annuity contracts once distributed from the plan.

Provide guidance on the extent of a fiduciary's duty in evaluating providers (e.g. insurance companies). He noted that ERISA does not require fiduciaries to have a "crystal ball" and that the recent final regulations on selection of annuity providers for distributions from DC plans (29 C.F.R. § 2550.404a-4) are informative and an improvement over the regulations on selecting annuity providers (Interpretive Bulletin 95-1). He encouraged DOL to remove the requirement from its regulations that fiduciaries determine the financial viability of providers by requiring an evaluation as to their ability to pay benefits in the future. He noted that this is an unreasonable expectation of fiduciaries and is an unnecessary requirement in light of the extensive regulation of the insurance industry.

- Provide a safe harbor to allow plans sponsors to provide education on distribution options. He noted that DOL Interpretive Bulletin 96-1, which addresses when providing investment-related information to participants in the accumulation phase is investment education rather than investment advice for ERISA purposes, has been a success. He pointed out that this guidance does not apply to education on the distribution phase.

Mr. Hadley indicated that a formulaic safe harbor for purposes of selecting annuity providers would be more helpful than procedure-oriented guidance. He noted that "soft guidance" directing fiduciaries on what to consider was not helpful if they were not told what to do with the considerations. He stated that in general, fiduciary safe harbors should be as specific as possible. He also noted that the regulations under section 404(c) of ERISA may also be amended to provide safe harbors with respect to retirement income protection options.

Abigail Pancoast, Lincoln Financial Group,
Appearing for the American Council of Life Insurers (ACLI),
Chair of the Retirement Plans Committee

As set forth in the testimony, ACLI members offer income products to plans and to individuals for their IRAs. The testimony outlines a variety of different types of annuities as well as defines key terms. In addition, the testimony discusses factors considered in pricing and provides some background on insurance regulation. The testimony points out with respect to the annuities, the expense charges and expected profit are embedded in the price, not separately disclosed. The testimony points out the value and importance of annuities. ACLI encouraged support for the development of product innovation, including the incrementally purchased payout annuity and the Guaranteed Minimum Withdrawal Benefit (GMWB).

The ACLI testimony recognized as impediments to annuity utilization plan sponsor concerns about fiduciary liability, administrative issues, and lack of participant knowledge. The testimony set forth a number of suggestions for Council recommendations to DOL.

The testimony proposes that IB 96-1 be expanded to clarify that providing information about payout options is not investment advice, and that plan assets can be used to offer education on payout options.

The testimony proposed changes to the requirements for selecting annuity providers. ACLI noted that the area of concern regards the interpretation that the plan fiduciary is expected to evaluate the financial status of the insurance company with ongoing liability for the financial security of the annuity provider. ACLI proposed an alternative that would provide a safe harbor where the plan fiduciary can rely on the insurance regulatory structure to analyze financial condition, and provide the public with assurance of the safety, of the insurance carrier. The testimony reviewed what state insurance regulators do to evaluate and monitor insurance carriers, and the value that brings.

The testimony supported illustrating the account balances as projected lifetime income on participant statements, and expressed appreciation that DOL is working on this issue.

ACLI noted that the issues surrounding the requirement for spousal consent on plan distributions complicate administration and requested that DOL issue guidance to ease the burdens.

Kelli Hueler
President and CEO, Hueler Companies

Kelli Hueler testified about a lifetime income product that was launched in 2004 called the Income Solutions® annuity program.® Under this program an individual can connect with a sponsoring organization to purchase an annuity after competitive bidding process which is as favorable as a group annuity. Ms. Hueler noted that the company offers the only nonexclusive, independent, institutional annuity platform available to plans. She noted that the platform has been adopted by some of the industry's largest plan administrators and plan sponsors, as well as key industry associations and fee for service advisors providing thousands of employer-sponsored plans access to the platform. Her testimony addressed five things to think in response to Council questions: (1) participant risks and considerations; (2) sponsor risks and considerations; (3) how to facilitate adoption of retirement income–structural and active guidance; (4) barriers; and (5) competition and transparency.

Ms. Hueler testified that plan sponsors are very concerned about fiduciary risk and that the selection of insurance companies is a major issue for plan sponsors and individuals. She stated that the company uses financial data, including rating agency information, and obtain help from an outside service to screen insurance companies with quarterly updates. She noted that thepurchase process is designed to present individuals with fair and unbiased information, to provide answers to questions, and to help e potential buyers understand the product. In addition, she discussed the importance of competitive pricing, transparency and fee disclosure.

Ms. Hueler noted that the information and tools built into the system architecture is "structural guidance" and question answering by a salaried employee of a program, a partner, or of the Hueler Company is "active guidance." She noted that in her experience the majority of buyers have questions that they want to have answered by a person and that the conversation that takes place is very important to the purchaser. She noted that while structural guidance is very important, it is not enough. Ms. Hueler stated that as part of the structural guidance that suitability reviews were incorporated into the process allowing information on buyers to be provided to purchasers. The reviews show that when people buy annuities, they usually use 20% to 25% of their assets for the purchase.

In her testimony, Ms. Hueler stated that additional barriers to, and support of, annuity purchase are often found in the communication with participants, and may even be related to conflicts of interest. She stated that she and other members of her staff have listened to recorded calls, and in some firms, annuity purchase is presented fairly and encouraged, while in others the participant is directed to another option. According to her experience when people buy annuities, they usually use 20% to 25% of their assets, and many of the purchases are after the participant leaves the plan.

Ms. Hueller noted that the three key participant risks and good reasons for annuitization are (1) investment risk, (2) longevity risk and (3) inflation risk. She further noted that the needs of participants vary by their life stages. In her work Ms. Hueler focuses on people who are transitioning to retirement and who are in retirement and noted that if the investment markets produce poor returns early in retirement that it is often a major issue for retirees.

The question was asked about whether today's low interest rates make annuities more expensive and Ms. Hueler responded that while prices have increased, annuities still offer a very good value compared to fixed income assets in the marketplace. She noted that yields on all types of fixed income investments have dropped dramatically.

Allison Klausner

General Counsel of Benefits at Honeywell International, testifying on behalf of American Benefits Council ("ABC")

Ms. Klausner testified regarding the fiduciary barriers, and the disclosure and education needs relating to income replacement or lifetime income products from the perspective of employer or plan sponsor. She stressed that offering employee benefit retirement plans is a voluntary system and any mandates or requirements imposed on employers could be burdensome, causing some employer to cease offering such benefits. Ms. Klausner stated that disclosure and education should be encouraged, not mandated. She noted that if DC plans were required to include an in-plan annuity vehicle as an investment fund such inclusion could create administrative complexities, challenging fiduciary obligations, and new and increased plan fees and costs which would more likely than not be borne by the plan participants.

Ms. Klausner stated that the most significant obstacle plan sponsors face providing an income stream for life is fiduciary concerns. The selection of an annuity provider is a source of significant potential liability and in the absence of employee demand for income replacement products it is hard for companies to incur this potential liability. She recommended that to overcome this obstacle, plan sponsors need clear, simple, fiduciary guidance allowing them to make lifetime income options available to plan participants without potential fiduciary liabilities. She stated that the DOL's Interpretive Bulletin 95-1 does not apply to the selection of an annuity contract for distributions from a DC plan. She recommended that DOL provide a safe harbor that would address the fiduciary liability concerns that plan sponsors currently have if they inform participants about the availability of the annuity platform for roll-overs IRAs, without any endorsement that would imply fiduciary responsibility. She also recommended that Interpretive Bulletin 96-1 be used as a template for developing rules and guidance with regard to distribution education.

She noted that an employer's approach to total retirement security is based on many factors including: types of plans offered - DC vs. DB; employee demographics; benchmark comparisons to other companies; portability of benefits; changes in participant circumstances; and changes in business operations.

During the Q&A session, Ms. Klausner was asked about inquiries from retirees or near-retirees about their concerns about distributions. She indicated that participants and retirees were more concerned about the taxation of the distributions or the fact that they have to take a distribution at a certain age. She indicated that she was not aware of anyone at her company that has asked about an investment in an annuity option regarding their DC plan.

Kevin T. Hanney
Direct of Portfolio Investments
United Technologies Corporation Pension Investments Group ("UTC").

Kevin Hanney provided testimony regarding obstacles facing plan sponsors when offering income replacement products. He noted that UTC provided several retirement plans, including a cash balance DB plan and a traditional DB plan. He stated that UTC embarked on developing a new retirement option, within the DC plan, that is designed specifically for the purpose of replacing income in retirement called the "lifetime income strategy." This product , he noted, was designed to improve the probability of a participant reaching his or her desired level of retirement income. Mr. Hanney shared with the Council that out of 100,000 participants, approximately 5,000 have investment elections in the lifetime income strategy to-date, with additional calls expressing interest and seeking more specific information on the product.

In summary, the lifetime income strategy is a target date investment strategy using an investment advisor to determine where it makes sense to begin purchasing units in group annuity contracts. It operates similarly to an individual variable annuity but with several providers. Mr. Hanney shared with the Council how important it was to understand that in providing any income replacement solution that there needs to be a considerable effort on the part of the employer and professionals to evaluate the solution and determine whether it is appropriate for the plan participants He noted that this is a significant obstacle for many plan sponsors, especially smaller companies. To help further alternatives options, Mr. Hanney recommended the following actions that could be taken:

- Establish clear but flexible guidance from all regulatory agencies to promote the development and adoption of income replacement solutions.
- Recognize that overly proscriptive standards will stymie innovation, reduce competition, and fail to meet the needs of a broad range of plans and participants.
- Update language in existing guidance to reflect recent product developments and innovations so fiduciaries can understand what is covered by existing guidance and safe harbor provisions.
- Define the characteristics of a qualified retirement income alternative with sufficient breadth so as to capture not only the products and services which function as the direct source of retirement income, but also to address their integration within the retirement vehicles and portfolio construction strategies.

Mr. Hanney stated that the regulatory agencies are in a position to provide the necessary level of competence to plan fiduciaries by issuing and clearly communicating, a process-focused standard of care for the evaluation, selection, and monitoring of income replacement solutions and service providers. He noted that a safe harbor to shield fiduciaries from costly lawsuits and potential liability would be appropriate.

During the Q&A session, Mr. Hanney was asked how the concerns over the safe harbor were overcome with the implementation of the lifetime income strategy. He stated that UTC believed that even if its interpretation of the safe harbor was optimistic, that the standard of care under ERISA in general was something it would seek to exceed.

Cynthia Mallett

Vice President for Industry Strategies & Public Policy, Corporate Benefit Funding Division, Metlife

Ms. Cynthia Mallet discussed MetLife's recently released study entitled "Perspectives of Plan Sponsors and Recordkeepers for Qualified Plans." The study, which surveyed 12 of the largest DC plan record keepers and 215 plan sponsors offering DB plans and/or DC plans, was intended to assist plan sponsors and record keepers to identify plan participants' retirement needs and to devise retirement income solutions under their DC plans. She noted the importance of this focus because of the continued shift from DB to DC pension plans, and the need for DC plans to evolve from supplemental savings plans to primary, or in some cases the only, employer -provided retirement plans for many workers. Ms. Mallett noted that a shift in focus from solely assets accumulation to include income distribution is critical for participants to best determine their retirement income needs, gain access the tools and solutions to generate guaranteed income in retirement.

The study explored the dynamics of the plan sponsor and record keeper relationship and the efforts being made to provide participants with the necessary education, tools, awareness and solutions, as well as identifying the perceived obstacles to providing retirement income options under DC plans. Under the study, 81% of plan sponsors reported that plan participants have the ability to make retirement income projections. But only 28% of plan sponsors stated that projections were automatically shown to participants when they viewed their account balances on-line, and only thirteen of the plan sponsors include retirement income projections on participant statements.

Ms. Mallett stated that changing the plan's ultimate focus and goal is the driver for determining whether retirement savings and retirement income are primary goals of plan participants. Under the study, 91% of plan sponsors concluded that accumulation of retirement savings is the primary focus of their DC plans, and only 9% of plan sponsors stated that retirement income and distribution is a primary focus. Ms. Mallett stated that learning from the study more participants would like a focus on lifetime income but is offered by few plan sponsors. She noted that record keepers and plan sponsors agreed that retirement income will be the biggest issue under DC plans in the years ahead.

In her testimony, Ms. Mallett noted that the current legal standards do not provide plan sponsors sufficient protection to offer retirement income solutions, and noted they are concerned about their ERISA fiduciary obligations in this area. She testified that safe harbors would be both welcomed and helpful, and suggested building on the existing participant disclosure rules. In addition, she proposed expanding IB 96-1 to clarify what information could be provided to educate participants without being characterized as fiduciary advice.

Ms. Mallett also suggested that DOL take a fresh look at the fiduciary duties surrounding the selection of annuity providers who offer lifetime income products to plan participants. She noted that 79% of the plan sponsors surveyed stated that fiduciary liability concerns discourage them from more widespread offering of income annuities within their DC plans.

Richard Pretty
Senior Managing Director and Product Actuary
TIAA-CREF

Mr. Pretty testified about the importance of lifetime annuities and lifetime guarantees as DB plans have become less available to employees. He noted that the insurance industry is responding with the development of an array of products. Mr. Pretty stated that the options can be generally categorized as withdrawal income or lifetime income options, with each having advantages and disadvantages. He noted that the disadvantage of the withdrawal income option is the risk that you may outlive the underlying assets, and the disadvantage of the traditional lifetime annuity is relinquishing control of and access to the assets. This, he noted, could be important if there is an emergency for additional funds.

Mr. Pretty stated that a compromise option, the Guaranteed Living Withdrawal Benefit, assures a lifetime benefit with access to cash, but noted that the lifetime benefit is reduced if you access the cash. He noted that a person with a retirement fund of 50% equity and 50% fixed income who retires with a plan to withdraw 5% a year has a greater than 20% chance of depleting the fund within 30 years. As Mr. Pretty stated, this needs to be a concern especially with the realization that for a married couple age 65 there is a 25% to 40% likelihood that one of them will live 30 years.

He stated that for a participant thinking of retirement, the following considerations are relevant: longevity risk, inflation risk, rising health care cost risk, investment return risk (particularly losses in the first years of retirement) and cognitive risk (the risk of mental inability to deal with finances in later life). He pointed out that lifetime income annuities address a number of these considerations. He noted that for the plan sponsor, there is a concern that providing an in-plan lifetime income option has a fiduciary obligation with respect to the selection of the institution of the provider of the lifetime income. He stated that a safe harbor provided by regulation would provide comfort to plan sponsors who would like to provide lifetime income options. He noted that another fiduciary concern for plan sponsors is assessing the costs of products they offer.

Mr. Pretty testified that TIAA-CREF offers a variety of online and individual interactive educational programs. He noted that changing the focus from accumulation of savings to retirement income (distribution) is critical to achieving better retirement outcomes. He spoke about the TIAA-CREF approach, noting that they start early with employees. He said the company has them set income goals and then project with them whether they are on track to meet those goals (using red, green and yellow lights to illustrate it). He noted that TIAA-CREF is seeing 25% to 40% of retirees choosing lifetime income options for at least a portion of their savings because of their educational programs. He pointed out that online projection tools are useful as an educational tool but should not be one dimensional. The tools should provide an array of assumptions that the employee can use in making the projections so they can see a range of outcomes.

The sooner an individual starts contributing to what ultimately would be their long-term guaranteed income the better that outcome will be as opposed to delaying the projection and decision making until they reach retirement.

Srinivas Reddy
Senior Vice President, Institutional Income
Prudential Retirement

Mr. Reddy testified that in-plan retirement income options have been slow to keep pace without-of-plan options, but that they are increasing. He noted that plan sponsors face the following challenges with respect to offering lifetime income solutions: assessing insurers' long term viability, comparing new and innovative products, educating workers and dealing with product portability.

He stated that on the viability issue, sponsors should be able to rely on state regulators who deal with this issue. Further, he said that DOL should clarify the regulations, and in a way that will not stifle innovation. With respect to comparing new products, he noted that sponsor anxiety will be alleviated over time as they become more familiar with the offerings. With regard to education, he stated that sponsors are concerned with the regulatory distinction of education vs. advice. He requested that DOL amend or supplement IB 96-1 to address this concern.

Through guidance, Mr. Reddy said DOL should condition participants to think in terms of future income, not just accumulation. The guidance, he stated, should encourage the use of lifetime income calculators. He shared that in Prudential's experience, when workers use calculators, they increase their deferral rates. With respect to portability, he stated that most providers can accommodate the transfer of lifetime income products from the 401(k) to the IRA and that work is progressing in providing for portability from one plan to another. He said that Prudential found that participants who opt for retirement income solutions defer 38% more income, were better diversified and were 2.5 time more likely to stay the course during volatile investment periods.

He stated that showing employees, through use of a calculator, how much lifetime income their rate of savings will generate results in an increased amount of savings. He spoke about one competitor having a mechanism to show persons in a certain profession what portion of their income their peers are saving. This, he notes, also generates greater savings.

He noted that lack of participant focus on the importance of lifetime income for retirement leads to lack of diversity in investment, low deferral rates and loss aversion. He cited the results of a study conducted by Prudential, where 40% of participants over 50 years of age were invested 100% in equities or 100% in fixed income. These problems lead to delayed retirement, higher health care costs for employers, and a decreased ability for plan sponsors to predict and plan for retirements.

He said when it comes to actually putting money in a guaranteed income product, Prudential recommends to participants to start doing it ten years before their targeted retirement, noting that in a ten-year horizon they have not seen a market that has performed worse than what the cost of the guarantee would be. Prudential believes that is not a risk participants can afford to take within ten years.

He said that the industry is a far way off from having capacity issues in handling participant shift to lifetime retiree income products. He noted that there are insurance products with regard to possible adverse longevity risks; that DOL can help in education efforts through clear regulations on the status of annuities and education vs. investment advice. Moreover, eductation efforts should encourage the use of projection tools and teach participants how to annuitize.

Richard Bailey, FSA, MAAA
VALIC

Mr. Bailey stated that retirement income is much more challenging for individuals than asset accumulation because of the unknowns: how long they will live and what their expenses will be. He noted that here are three choices available to the individual: manage their distributions, purchase annuities, or some combination of both. With the option of managing their distributions, he stated that there is no guarantee they will not outlive their income. An option, he noted, could be to allocate income distributions based on a projection of a very long life, but that would reduce the amount of yearly income and still not guarantee that the individual will not outlive their money, even when meeting investment targets.

He spoke with respect to the guaranteed income side, noting that there are products that allow persons to use conservative assumptions and accept a lower initial income amount, thereby increasing the chances that they will be protected against later inflation. He spoke of the option that permits the participant to choose investing a part of his/ her assets in an annuity and manage the remaining funds.

He noted that longevity products involve a pooling of the longevity risk. He said that one reason DB plans have declined is that employees undervalue them in the same way that participants undervalue and underutilize lifetime income products. He said that the complexity of longevity products, the under-appreciation of longevity risk, and the difficulty in determining how much retirement income will be needed, are factors that contribute to this undervaluation.

He pointed out that there's a significant gap in the income options available and utilized in DC plans compared with those more available in the marketplace. He noted that there is an even wider gap between participants' knowledge on managing income in retirement and what most experts advise them to learn. He stated that too often, employees contribute to their 401(k) only up to the amount their employer is matching because they do not know how much they should save to provide adequate income replacement in retirement. He noted that individuals need tools to help them determine how much they should save.

Mr. Bailey stated if individuals have a guaranteed income, where they were actually giving up all liquidity and all of the cash values currently, that there is certainly greater leverage in purchasing something earlier because, in a case of 10,000 people there is an acceptance of some greater risk of dying too soon in terms of greater leverage against the risk of living too long. He noted that with respect to the possibility of adverse longevity experience, life insurers are in a much better position to handle this.

Jason Scott
Managing Director
Financial Engines Retiree Research Center.

Dr. Scott stated that Financial Engines, through its services and its partners, assists 8 million 401(k) plan participants, generally in large plans, with investing and planning for retirement. He stated that Financial Engines devises portfolios and manages portfolios for 600,000 participants with the median participant client having a $40,000 account balance. The company recently introduced a retirement income service called "Income Plus" that offers flexible, stable payouts that participants can choose to make last for life.

In his testimony, Dr. Scott made the following observations:

First, that DC plans have a big role to play in retirement income due to their lower costs, general access to service providers, and efficacy. He defined efficacy to include, the success of plans, through defaults, in increasing participation rates, saving rates and investment allocation diversification. He supported the use of defaults on the retirement income (decumulation) front.

Second, that workable lifetime income solutions must meet the needs of both participants and plan sponsors. He observed that 401(k) plans are built around choice, both in terms of sponsors offering a plan and participants choosing to use it. With respect to retirement income, he noted that his research indicates that participants value:

- Income payments that are stable over time with no major declines (Safety)
- Income payments that can last for life (Safety)
- Protection from poor market performance before and during retirement (Safety)
- No irrevocable commitments. Ability to reverse any decision (Control / Flexibility)
- Access and control of assets at all times (Control / Flexibility)

Maintaining access and control, he noted, is especially important to retirees and stated that for lifetime income solutions to be successful in DC plans that participants must be allowed to maintain control of their retirement assets while still receiving income.

He noted that plan sponsors often take the following positions with respect to retirement income solutions:

- They must be operationally easy to add to the plan without complex and costly changes and added measures.
- They must be easily removable to accommodate changing needs of the participants and to avoid the locked-in feeling.
- There must be clear application of fiduciary responsibilities and avoidance of legal or regulatory uncertainty.
- Sponsors want to avoid conflicts of interest.
- Sponsors do not want high or hidden costs.

Third, Dr. Scott stated that current regulations should consider participant flexibility to retain control. In addition, he noted that participants can improve their financial situation by delaying their receipt of Social Security benefits and using their 401(k) accounts to provide income in the interim.

Stephen Sexauer
Chief Investment Officer, AGI Solutions

Stephen Sexauer provided testimony on behalf of Allianz Global Investors Solutions. He framed his testimony to answer the overarching question: how can we create almost guaranteed income in a largely Defined Contribution (DC) world to replace the Defined Benefit (DB) plan.

Mr. Sexauer stated that he did not see DC plans as the solution to retirement income that many people believed them to be because: 1) the coverage rate for DB plans never covered the entire population and 2) some DB plans were poorly managed, leaving participants with inadequate protection or minimal benefits paid through the PBGC, noting that the failure of some plans has been catastrophic for those not covered by Social Security. He also noted that the dominant source of retirement income for the majority of Americans will be Social Security benefits and that both DB and DC plans are important secondary supplements.

He stated that DC plans leave participants with the difficult task of figuring out how to turn account balances into lifetime income. He suggested that participants need professional calculations to translate their account balances into a steady stream of income. He pointed out that there is no risk-free solution to retirement income. He noted that it helps to point outthe decisions involved in managing the risks in order to get retirees to where they need to be. However, longevity pooling is necessary and provides large gains and up to 30% fewer assets needed to fund a given level of retirement income.

Mr. Sexauer noted that the five dominant risks are not saving enough; longevity risk or outliving savings; investment risk including inflation risk; counterparty risk; and liquidity risk. He suggested that people need professional advice in figuring out how much to save, access to longevity pooling, inflation-protected income and clarity about the costs of various options.

Mr. Sexauer made the following recommendations: (1) Continuously promote increased savings with good participant choice and incentive; (2) Develop a public benchmark to permit for default asset allocations and risks profile; (3) Create a lifetime income safe harbor; (4) Provide sufficient public and employer-provided participant education to help them make informed choices; (5) Provide clear guidance in rules and regulatory form to allow plan sponsor to more widely embrace offering lifetime income options to their participants.

Julie Mix McPeak

Commissioner of Insurance for the State of Tennessee; Chair of the National Association of Insurance Commissioners Life Insurance and Annuities Committee

Commissioner McPeak provided testimony on behalf of the National Association of Insurance Commissioners (NAIC)'s Life Insurance and Annuities (A) Committee regarding the state insurance regulators' oversight of the life insurance and annuities industry. She stated that life insurance companies are subject to stringent laws and regulations, and that state insurance regulators have broad authorities to identify and address issues before they threaten an insurer's solvency or otherwise pose an issue for the protection of policyholder interests. Her testimony focused on the insurance regulation's financial solvency framework, insurance company receivership and market conduct regulation regarding consumer protections. Ms. McPeak stated that it is the responsibility of state insurance regulators to protect policyholders and to ensure a healthy competitive market for insurance products. She also indicated that NAIC is in the process of forming a working group to consider the soundness of the annuity providers as part of DOL's safe harbor provisions.

Insurance Regulation's Financial Solvency Framework: Under this structure, issuers are required to be licensed in their state of domicile and in all other states where their products and services are sold. A critical component of the regulatory system is detailed and transparent reporting and disclosure requirements. Another important aspect is the emphasis that is place on capital standards. The NAIC risk-based capital (RBC) system serves as a safety net for insurers, is uniform among states, and provides regulatory authority for timely action. State insurance investment laws limit on the amount and type of investments insurers can make in an effort to limit the company's risk exposure.

Ms. McPeak also described the minimum valuation and reserve requirements for life insurance policies and contracts which are defined in the "Standard Valuation Law" and adopted by all 50 states. She noted that life insurers are also subject to periodic stress tests involving an annual cash flow testing exercise designed to test the company's resilience to specific interest rate scenarios, as well as other financial requirements.

Insurance Company Receivership: Ms. McPeak discussed the receivership process and the ramifications to policyholders. She stated that in the case of an insolvent insurer the receivership laws of the state give policyholders priority over most claimants, with state guaranty funds to serve as a backstop if the insured does not have sufficient funds.

Market Conduct Regulation: Ms. McPeak stated that regulators also have broad authorities to police the conduct of insurers and agents. To further this goal, she noted that the NAIC took specific steps to ensure the suitability of the annuity for the consumer, citing a few examples.

During the Q&A session, Ms. McPeak was asked about the state guaranty fund and how it applies to a particular contract. She indicated that the consumer (under both individual and group annuities) is required to purchase an annuity in the state where they reside –residency governs the guaranty for the annuity. She noted that products are approved on a state-by-state basis. Also, she noted that guaranty coverage varies by state and type of product but can range from $100,000 to $500,000.

She also said that the states have a prohibition on discussing the existence of a Guaranty Association at the insurance agent or company level at the time an insurance transaction is being conducted. After the purchase is made, some states allow notification while other states mandate notification of the existence of a Guaranty Association. She stated that it has long been the historical perspective of insurance regulators that insurance consumers should not have to rely on the existence of a Guaranty Association when deciding to purchase an insurance product, including an annuity. Rather, she noted, the industry would rather consumers look at other factors such as the rating associations of insurance companies and the financial stability of a company. When questioned about appropriate standard for a safe harbor for plan sponsors and fiduciaries with respect to selecting providers of annuity, Ms. McPeak noted that they should not rely solely on the fact that a company is licensed in a state, but should also take into account the significant oversight by State and some of the factors used in this process.

End Notes

[1] See testimony of Bruce Ashton, Drinker Biddle & Reath LLP; Michael Hadley, Davis & Harmon LLP; Article: Lifetime Income in Defined Contribution Plans: A Fiduciary Approach (A White Paper by Fred Reish, Bruce Ashton and Joseph Faucher)

[2] §2550.404a-4

Selection of annuity providers –safe harbor for individual account plans.

(a) Scope. (1) This section establishes a safe harbor for satisfying the fiduciary duties under section 404(a)(1)(B) of the Employee Retirement Income Security Act of 1974 (ERISA), 29 U.S.C. 1104-11, in selecting an annuity provider and contract for benefit distributions from an individual account plan.

(b) Safe harbor. The selection of an annuity provider for benefit distributions from an individual account plan satisfies the requirements of section 404(a)(1)(B) of ERISA if the fiduciary:

(1) Engages in an objective, thorough and analytical search for the purpose of identifying and selecting providers from which to purchase annuities;

(2) Appropriately considers information sufficient to assess the ability of the annuity provider to make all future payments under the annuity contract;

(3) Appropriately considers the cost (including fees and commissions) of the annuity contract in relation to the benefits and administrative services to be provided under such contract;

(4) Appropriately concludes that, at the time of the section, the annuity provider is financially able to make all future payments under the annuity contract and the cost of the annuity contract is reasonable in relation to the benefits and services to be provided under the contract; and

(5) If necessary, consults with an appropriate expert or experts for purposes of compliance with the provisions of this paragraph (b).

[3] Interpretive Bulletin 95-1 set forth in general that ERISA's standard of prudence required that a plan fiduciary select the safest available annuity provider, unless under the circumstances it would be in the interest of the participants and beneficiaries to do otherwise. The Bulletin also provided general guidance when it may be in the interest of the participants and beneficiaries to purchase other than the safest available annuity.

[4] Board of Trustees, Federal Old-age and Survivors Insurance and Federal Disability Insurance Trust Funds, 2012 Annual Report of the Board of Trustees of the Federal Old-Age and Survivors Insurance and Federal Disability Insurance Trust Funds 91 (tbl. V.A4) (2012)

[5] Robert F. Fogel, *Forward: Towrad and Era of Longevity and Wealth*, in Lessons From Pension Reform In the Americas 1, 4 (Stephen J. Kay & Tapen Sinha, eds., 2008)

[6] More detailed chart provided by TIAA-CREF included in the Appendix.

[7] Society of Actuaries 2012 Decision Briefs

INDEX

A

B

C

D

E

I

J

L

M

N

O

P

Q

R

S

Y